THE SECRET CHURCH

THE TREASURE OF RENNES-LE-CHATEAU

BY

GEOFFREY MORGAN

Bloomington, IN  Milton Keynes, UK

authorHOUSE®

AuthorHouse™
1663 Liberty Drive, Suite 200
Bloomington, IN 47403
www.authorhouse.com
Phone: 1-800-839-8640

AuthorHouse™ UK Ltd.
500 Avebury Boulevard
Central Milton Keynes, MK9 2BE
www.authorhouse.co.uk
Phone: 08001974150

First published by AuthorHouse 11/2/2006

ISBN: 1-4259-6945-3 (sc)

Printed in the United States of America
Bloomington, Indiana

This book is printed on acid-free paper.

Dedication

To the memory of my dear wife Doreen.

Contents

LIST OF ILLUSTRATIONS

Plate – 1
Is of the hilltop village of Rennes-le-Chateau, the author at the door of St
Mary Magdalene, the priest Berenger Sauniere and his housekeeper Marie
Denarnaud.

Plate 2
Shows the Villa Bethanie, the Church, the statue of Asmodeus, Sauniere's
grave and headstone at Rennes-le-Chateau.

Plate 3
The first picture is of the stone boulder armchair on the hillside just south
of Rennes les Bains. It is the *chair* used by Sauniere in his statue of
Asmodeus.
The second picture is of the so-called *Visigoth pillar* that once formed part
of the Altar in Sauniere's church and in which he discovered the concealed
Parchments.
Picture number three is of the ornate *Apprentice's pillar* in Rosslyn Chapel
and the last picture is a facsimile of *Parchment Two*, one of which was
found in the Altar pillar.

Plate 4
This plate includes the picture of the Cathar fortress of *Montsegur*,
Sauniere's fortified library, the *Tour Magdala* and the author stood at the
Menhir or *Standing Stone* with Cardou in the background.

Plate 5
There are two pictures to this plate, the first is of the *Fleury Tableau* which
is on the west wall of St Mary Magdalene and the second is of Nicolas
Poussin's painting *Les Berger's d'Arcadie* (The Arcadian Shepherds).

Plate 6
The first picture was taken from the Tour Magdala and shows the
church tower of St Mary Magdalene with the high hill *Cardou* in the
background.
The second shows the middle hill *Auriol* and the last is of the low hill *Bois
du Lauzet*.

Plate 7 ...

Has two pictures; the one is of *St Nazaire Et Celse* which was taken from across the River Sals at Rennes les Bains – the second is *within the church* showing the modern Altar on which are noteworthy symbols.

Plate 8 ...

The top photograph is of the bridge at *Rennes les Bains* that is at the convergence of the rivers Blanche and Sals at the pool known as the Holy Water Stoup.

The second picture is of the site of the old *Tomb of Arques* at Pontils.

Plate 9

This is a composite picture of part of the sketch map of Pontils showing the Tomb of Arques and the Standing stone. It is the place where Nicolas Poussin painted *Les Berger's d'Arcadie* (the Arcadian shepherds). The radiating lines pick out the salient features, which may be recognised in the painting.

Plate 10

This plate is similar in character to Plate 9 but the location is at Rennes les Bains

Plate 11 ...

On this plate we see the *Altar* that Sauniere built in St Mary Magdalene and pictures of *Stations of the Cross, No's 1* and *XIV.*

Plate 12 ...

On this plate we have a picture of the *Sacristy* at Rosslyn Chapel, a view of the Alleyway leading to St Nazaire Et Celse with the old Presbytery on the left. The carving of part of the *danse macabre* in the Lady Chapel, also at Rosslyn and the *Knight's Tombstone*, which Sauniere reputedly recovered from the church floor of St Mary Magdalene.

CHAPTER 1
THE LURE OF GOLD

Little in this world of ours awakens mans innate quest, his apparent oblivion to everything else around him more than the lure of gold ... treasure, buried treasure! Berenger Sauniere the Priest of Rennes-le-Chateau was no exception. From as early as he could recall there had been stories of hidden treasure. His parents, his grand parents and their parents before them were no strangers to the rumours that from time to time would circulate in the neighbourhood.

The River Rialsesse that flows past Arques and the Tomb of Arques to join with the Sals west of Serres is known as the River of the Kings Gold and which is linked with Poussin's painting of *Midas washing himself in the Pactolus*. Whilst there may be nothing to substantiate any rumour that gold had been found in the Railsesse, to the young ears of Berenger Sauniere bygone stories of gold having been found in the river resulting in an intense hunt along the dried up riverbed during the summer months would further excite him. Such tall stories are largely forgotten with the passage of time, but the young impressionable Sauniere was excited by the thoughts of treasure and whenever the opportunity arose to question his peers on the subject he would do so. Slowly and surely with the passage of time his certainty of treasure in the area grew and ever more pointed him in the direction of Rennes-le-Chateau.

Berenger Sauniere was born in 1852 in the village of Montazels, close to Couiza within the Upper Aude Valley and only a few kilometres from where his exploits would ensure him and it a lasting place in history. He was the first child of many, of who much was expected. He did not disappoint his parents and studied for the priesthood, being ordained in 1879. After two earlier appointments lasting six years he became Parish Priest of Rennes-le-Chateau in 1885 at the age of 33 years. Following a political setback he was forced to leave his post, but his representations to the authorities paid off and one year after his original appointment he was once more back at St. Mary Magdalene as the incumbent of the Parish of Rennes-le-Chateau. Those who knew the poor state of both Church and living on that remote hilltop must surely have raised the question, why was Sauniere so keen to return after rejecting a promising appointment in the Seminary at Narbonne. Call it what you will, but Berenger Sauniere had a vision a gut feeling cultivated during the earlier years that convinced him his destiny lay at Rennes-le-Chateau. He was not to be proven wrong. On becoming Priest in this remote hamlet Sauniere inherited the services of a young woman named Marie Denarnaud who was to be his housekeeper and companion and who would play an important and vital role during the years he lived in the Village.

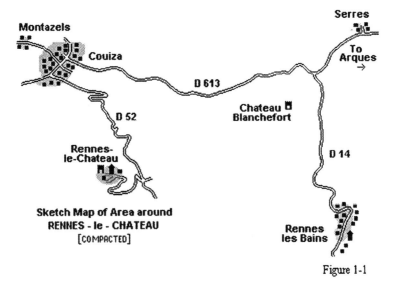

Sketch Map of Area around
RENNES - le - CHATEAU
[COMPACTED]

Figure 1-1

The young priest was poorly paid and his church was in a desperate state of repair. With the benevolence of a few of his more wealthy parishioners money was eventually obtained for limited works of restoration and to support his living. In 1891, five years after much toil a devastating storm caused further damage to the Church. The story goes that part of the structure of the church roof fell and struck the Altar. In attempting to straighten his Communion table Sauniere discovered that one of the pillars of the Altar was hollow and reaching inside he found a sealed wooden tube. That pillar is now in the Presbytery Museum at Rennes-le-Chateau and although the stone is inverted to prevent further damage to the recess it is clear to anyone studying the carving on that pillar that its unusual and strange symbols in the design would have attracted the priest's attention, adding fuel to his belief in the existence of a treasure. Whether or not the collapse of part of the building was responsible for the alleged displacement of the Altar must remain open to question. Sauniere had often contemplated the meaning of the odd characters the mason had carved on the Altar pillar and by adopting the pose of the second symbol was beginning to understand its meaning and consequently its significance. It was clear what was intended and not difficult to complete the scene once the storm had set the stage. It is my belief that it was at this time when Sauniere was resetting his Communion table that he discovered the underside of the stone slab tabletop to his Alter was inscribed with an unusual and mysterious design. The slab, which is now referred to as the *Grave Slab* was sketched by him and then thought subsequently destroyed.

The story of the priest finding a wooden tube containing Parchments in one of the hollowed out Altar pillars is well documented and facsimiles of the Parchments may be seen in most books on the subject of the Treasure of Rennes-le-Chateau.

Rennes-le-Chateau

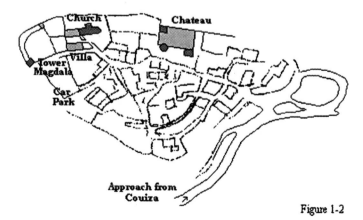

Figure 1-2

The tale is not without the sceptics and official denials that the priest ever discovered a treasure. The story is further aggravated by the

3

introduction of the so-called Codes and Ciphers. These are seen as a diversion, a cleverly contrived trick, which is admitted by some as 'making no sense whatsoever'. And yet, copious amounts of time and energies have been spent on trying to resolve what amounts to be a meaningless jumble of words.

No conclusions have been reached, even if the Parchments are considered genuine as to the likely author of the documents. What is not in dispute is that Henry Lincoln who introduced the story to a wider public awareness has found encoded messages set amongst the text of the Parchments.

In addition to the parchments and what on the face of it is an integral part of the story, is the enigmatic painting by Nicolas Poussin entitled Les Berger's d'Arcadie, or the Arcadian Shepherds. The association, if indeed it is to be considered as having a bearing on the tale, has never been properly assessed.

As to the likely sequence of events that led to the priest locating the treasure, and it is not denied that Berenger Sauniere spent huge sums of money on property, his church and an extravagant life style has also never been properly explored. This applies particularly to the *clues* the priest has bequeathed us in his statues and Stations of the Cross in the church of St Mary Magdalene.

Berenger Sauniere began his time at Rennes-le-Chateau in abject poverty and ended his days on that remote hilltop a penniless defrocked priest. In the intervening years his fortune and his secret, which went with him to his grave, became legendary.

The story of his breakthrough relating to the treasure began late one afternoon when his bell ringer, on coming down the belfry steps discovered the top of the newel post to be loose. He removed the cap of the post and found a small glass bottle containing a fragment of parchment, which he handed to the priest. Whatever was on that parchment it led Sauniere to instruct his builders to excavate in the floor of the church, in front of the Altar. A stone slab was unearthed together with a few pieces of jewellery. This slab, which is different from the *Grave Slab,* became known as the, *Knights Tombstone* and is now in the Museum at Rennes-le-Chateau. It is rather strange that Sauniere should have preserved the tombstone, when the other, thought defaced by him was left shattered in the church grounds. Perhaps the *Knights Tombstone* was spared because the priest could not understand the relief pictures carved upon it and decided to keep it as a curio. If he had realised what the stone was telling him, things would have been so different.

News of the find under the church floor probably accounted for the priest's nighttimes digging in the churchyard, for which his Bishop admonished him, following letters of complaint by the parishioners of Rennes-le-Chateau. There is no record of what the priest was searching for or whether or not anything was discovered.

A full century has elapsed since the priest set out his clues to the treasure within the Church of Mary Magdalene and until now no one is any closer to solving the mystery. The stumbling block is the Codes and Ciphers attributed to either the Abbe Bigou or to a modern-day hoaxer and associated with the Parchments and a headstone purporting to be part of the grave furniture of Marie de Negri D'Hautpoul de Blanchefort who resided at Rennes-le-Chateau.

The priest took the Parchments he had discovered in the Altar pillar to his Bishop in Carcassonne, who dispatched him to Paris to seek verification of the Parchment's authenticity. Upon his return to Rennes-le-Chateau Sauniere reportedly brought with him three prints of paintings. They were, Poussin's *Les Berger's d'Arcadie* (The Arcadian Shepherds ... Louvre), the *St. Anthony Hermit* by Tenier and a Portrait of Pope Celestine.

The Paris researchers took a while before the findings were assessed and returned to the Bishop of Carcassonne. Sauniere had taken the precaution of having previously copied the Parchments and was able to study the documents at his leisure. He saw the raised letters above the lines on Parchment One and the symbol at the bottom of Parchment Two. He also recognised that the symbol on the second Parchment was in the form of a monogram, the 'signature' of the painter Nicolas Poussin. Sauniere may have known of the painting, *Les Berger's d'Arcadie* from his childhood days and that the painting depicted the *Tomb of Arques*, which was at Pontils on the road to Arques, a few kilometres from his home at Montazels. He recalled it well, having often crossed the stream by the road and clambered up the rocky promontory to the old tomb.

Now, within a few years of becoming the priest at Rennes-le-Chateau he was beginning to sense there were signs that he was on the track of something exciting. His problems though had only just begun. It was one thing to have the Parchments, the painting and the Grave slab, quite another to understand the symbols, the text, the coded messages and the purpose and the inscription on the *Tomb of Arques* as shown in the Painting. He desperately required guidance; a sign from the Almighty would help. "I wonder Lord if you could see your way clear to ... ". The answer was not immediately forthcoming; time passed and when it did arrive, to the priest's disappointment his plea was only answered in part. Even so, Sauniere's careful and meticulous work on the Parchments was paying off. He had decoded the cipher messages as Henry Lincoln has demonstrated and he understood the secret in Poussin's painting in association with Parchment One. He knew the Parchments were the work of the painter Nicolas Poussin and furthermore he was aware of the general direction in which he was being pointed. A Priest of Sauniere's calibre actively searching for a treasure he knew to be within his grasp was a man on a mission. Poussin had been very clever, he had set out his clues with much embroidery and many a strand going nowhere: or so it seemed. The priest realised the *Grave Slab* with its two different languages provided an important link in the chain to the treasure. However, the built-in confusion was pointing him in different directions. His breakdown of the word *Arcadia* that formed part of the inscription *Et In Arcadia Ego* in the painting, not only took him away from Rennes-le-Chateau, where he was convinced the treasure lay, it also made nonsense of the direction indicated by the Symbol on the top of Parchment One. ... Perhaps another word with the Lord might be in order.

The final breakthrough came after re-examining the Parchment Two symbol. The priest was learned in Latin with a smattering of Greek. He was also seeing what all modern commentators on the subject have overlooked. It was not his academic prowess that enabled him to triumph, but a simple observation. The Parchment Two symbol was more than a monogram it was a clever directional indicator and perfectly complimented the symbol on Parchment One. ... The priest of Rennes-le-Chateau knew where the treasure was located. It was time to sketch the inscriptions on the *Grave Slab* and then – so we are told, break the stone into a hundred pieces.

The painter had placed the Parchments in the Altar pillar circa 1646, when extensive renovation work was undertaken at St. Mary Magdalene. Berenger Sauniere has recorded this date on the right hand side of the entrance porch to *his* Church.

For two hundred and forty years a priest had stood before that Communion table and failed to realise the significance of the strange symbols on the pillar. It took the mind of Berenger Sauniere to search the depths of the mystery. The Altar is a place where the priest and his Lord meet to share the Sacraments, a Holy Symbol of the Church, which regardless of ones suspicions in its design was not to be desecrated. Poussin had chosen the placing of his clues carefully and in this case, in the certain knowledge that, 'even in the centuries to come', they would not be discovered he felt confident he had fulfilled his task.

Poussin was not to know that an *Act of God*, the very being he considered as guardian of his secret, would provide the opportunity for an errant priest to exploit the damage a storm had caused to the church of St Mary Magdalene, and thus to set in motion a chain of events that has been a quest for thousands and which is about to be revealed for all the world to see.

Following his discovery and after a period of time, Sauniere came to know within a few metres where the treasure was hidden and that as Poussin stated, *'It was only for the Priesthood'*. - Yet although a priest himself, there was no automatic passport to wealth. There was scheming to do, risks to take and a plan of campaign to be thought through. His solution was brilliant. In essence simple, offering an appearance of naiveté designed to deceive.

A scenario was imagined by the author, which may appeal to the reader as being plausible. It is an explanation that takes into account a number of reported *facts* of the case. It will be demonstrated that the entire evidence the priest had on which to base his assumption – the same evidence that is now available to the author of this work ... except that Sauniere knew the topography of his area, and it comprised only of the Altar pillars, the Parchments and Poussin's painting. With these items alone – and in my case, Henry Lincoln's excellent work in his book, 'The Holy Place', nothing else is required to locate the Treasure of Rennes-le-Chateau.

The situation is this: Sauniere knew where the treasure could be located and in his scheme all that was initially required was a reason for visiting his brother priest, the Abbe Henri Boudet at Rennes les Bains. He was to become interested in collecting rocks as it was known that one of Boudet hobbies was amateur geology; although for a while his activities in that field had been overtaken by work on his book. None the less it was an interest Sauniere hoped to reawaken in the older priest.

The plan he had formulated in his mind required an accomplice, one who would ask no questions and pose no threat. There was one person who fitted the role perfectly... his housekeeper Marie Denarnaud. At that time in 1892 Marie was an attractive 24-year-old who would be pleasant company for the Priest of Rennes-le-Chateau's older friend the Abbe Boudet. It would be customary for a priest visiting another parish to enter the church for prayer and personal devotion. Marie Denarnaud was to set about her task of occupying the older man's attention or by assisting Boudet's own elderly housekeeper in the preparation of a meal; that was the nub of Sauniere's plan.

The older priest, who was by now a little infirmed, would no doubt be thrilled with the company of the pretty woman who gave him every attention whilst Sauniere made his excuse to enter the church of St Nazaire Et Celse for his devotions.

Sauniere had guessed that if there was a way from within the building down under the church, where he felt sure the treasure laid, it could only accessed from one point. The message he had decoded from the Parchment was convincing enough … *'This treasure belongs to Dagobert II King and to Sion and he is there dead'*. – Buried beneath the church.

Sauniere had not visited the church of St Nazaire Et Celse for a number of years, but he could picture the layout within the building and felt confident, given the opportunity he could go directly to the place he was seeking.

Henri Jean Jacques Boudet was born in 1837 and was ordained into the priesthood when twenty-four years of age. His appointment to the post of Priest in the Parish of Rennes les Bains took place around 1872, where he stayed until failing health forced him out in 1914. Henri Boudet had been a keen walker, with literary ambitions and quite probably an amateur geologist. By 1892 however at the age of 54 years his energetic days were over and he spent more of his time writing his book on the Celtic language.

For a number of years the parishioners of Rennes les Bains had enjoyed the benevolence of their sometimes-generous priest. Few had questioned how on his meagre stipend his lifestyle and his spending appeared incompatible with that expected of a priest. It was something that may have crossed the minds of other priests in the vicinity, particularly Sauniere who was struggling to make ends meet.

It was an event that occurred shortly before the priest of Mary Magdalene was about to put his plan into effect that dramatically changed Sauniere's plans. It became common knowledge that the Abbe Boudet had at last published his book. Not that that in itself was to alert Sauniere's suspicions, but that Boudet had paid the high publishing cost with gold coins. Sauniere was now sure that he was not alone in knowing where the treasure was to be found and armed with his evidence he decided to confront Boudet. The meeting may have been a little uncomfortable for both men but Sauniere was well prepared and an amicable arrangement was agreed. It was to be the first of many visits by the priest of Rennes-le-Chateau and his housekeeper to Rennes les Bains.

The villagers of Rennes-le-Chateau had noticed that their priest and Marie were often away all day in the hills, returning home in the evening loaded with rocks. It appeared their man of God had embarked on a new adventure and soon they were bringing him offerings of stone to add to his mounting collection.

CHAPTER 2
EXPOUNDING A MYSTERY

Thirty years have passed since Henry Lincoln presented the BBC Chronicle films of the story of a poor French priest named Berenger Sauniere and the small hilltop village of Rennes-le-Chateau, which is situated at the foot of the Pyrenees. The tale of the priest, the village and the treasure associated with it has become legendary. It is a story of mystery and intrigue that has captured the imagination of television presenters and generated enough literature to fill a library. And yet, the source of the wealth that overnight changed the life of a penniless priest to one of riches beyond dreams has not been discovered ... until now!

Although from time to time through the intervening years since the 1970's I had not entirely forgotten the story my interest was once more awakened, when ten years ago I was presented with a copy of Henry Lincoln's book, 'The Holy Place'. I was soon engrossed in the book and became hooked on the romantic notions of solving the mystery and discovering the treasure. Such thoughts were quickly dashed after a few pages when I realised the enormity of the problem, which was compounded by my inability to comprehend the French and Latin languages; a prerequisite it seems to solving the complex Codes and Ciphers contained in the Parchments that the priest has uncovered and which Henry Lincoln had presented.

A few years after the villagers became aware that their priest had discovered the Parchments they noted he was spending large sums of money on property and an extravagant life style. The source of his wealth, which has become know as, *The Treasure of Rennes-le-Chateau* was as much a mystery then as it has remained unto this day.

In 1999 doubts were expressed in the BBC Time Watch programme, 'The History of a Mystery', featuring a book by Andrews and Schellenberger, entitled, 'The Tomb of God' that Sauniere, after he had found the Parchments had visited Paris. Before returning to Rennes-le-Chateau from the Capital he is said to have purchased copies of paintings by Poussin, Teniers and of the portrait of Pope Celestine V from the Louvre Museum. Whatever the truth of it, it is now only the *Poussin* painting that continues to play a significant role in the story.

There is no denying that the priest spent large sums of money in and around the village. What is in contention is the source of his wealth, upon which no one seems to agree. At the time his Bishop demanded to know where the money had come from and the priest was summoned to account for his sudden riches; something Sauniere refused to do. Marie Denarnaud, Sauniere's long time housekeeper is rumoured to have worn ancient gold rings and had told villagers that they were 'walking on gold', promising to reveal its whereabouts before she died. If she did know where the treasure lay, and it is most unlikely, her secret also went with her to the grave. Today the official Church's position is that there was no treasure, although no explanation is offered for the source of the large sums of money it is acknowledged the priest spent.

In 1656, during a visit to Rome, the Abbe Louis Fouquet called on Nicolas Poussin. The occasion may have been a matter of courtesy, the two having become acquainted when the painter was at the Court of Louis X1V of France in 1640; or else, the Abbe was aware that Poussin was engaged in intrigued and had hoped to gain from his visit.

Whatever the reason, it resulted in the Abbe writing a letter to his brother, who was the Superintendent of Finances at the Court, saying that Poussin possessed knowledge of the whereabouts of great wealth. The painter further stated that, *it is possible nobody else will ever rediscover* (the treasure) *in the centuries to come.* And that, *these things are so difficult to discover that nothing now on this earth can prove of better value nor be its equal.* (Lincoln). It seems likely that it was either the wine or Poussin's inflated ego which led him to divulge a great deal of information, particularly about *Les Berger's d'Arcadie* which King Louis acquired some time after the death of Cardinal Massimi in 1677. The King locked the painting away in his private rooms being convinced an important secret lay in the composition of the painting. The painting is now in the Louvre in Paris.

It emerged from Lincoln's and other writer's work, which are mainly based on Lincoln, that there were issues barring a way to the treasure that could not be resolved. These included the mystery surrounding Poussin's painting and the so-called Codes and Ciphers contained within the parchments, together with a headstone attributed to Marie de Negri D'Hautpoul de Blanchefort, whose remains are interred in the cemetery at Rennes-le-Chateau.

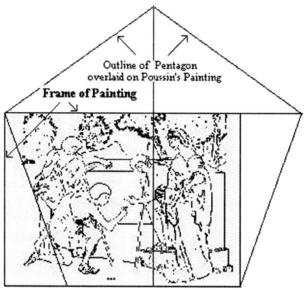

Part Sketch of Henry Lincoln's geometric overlay on Poussin's Les Bergers d'Arcadie

Figure 2-1

The Codes continue to be a stumbling block and although Henry Lincoln has done much in decoding the hidden messages in Parchments One and Two, no one has yet made sense of the resulting bizarre and meaningless jumble of words revealed in the text of the parchments. Lincoln had noticed that lines could be drawn through certain letters in the text and symbols on Parchment One and which he developed into geometric designs. These were then, following professional advice, introduced to the painting as a superimposed drawing in the form of a pentagon. This drawing appears to rely on the frame of Poussin's picture for its principal coordinates, which is hardly a basis to inspire confidence in the theory, considering that the picture was painted long before it was framed. The story in Lincoln's book *The Holy Place* was beginning to lose its appeal. If the priest had discovered a treasure I failed to understand how it was he needed radiating lines over huge tracts of land involving reference to the Paris Meridian, all requiring expensive maps and travel beyond the means of a penniless priest. I felt that the treasure was in the vicinity of the place that gives it its present day title and that if it was not at Rennes-le-Chateau, it was within walking distance of that place; something that is picked up by Stanley James in his Book 'The Treasure Maps of Rennes-le-Chateau'. Indeed, Sauniere's parishioners were aware their *man of God* could be seen setting out early in the day accompanied by his housekeeper and arriving home late in the evenings laden with 'rocks', at a point in time when Sauniere's wealth began to materialize. As well as reports of Marie Denarnaud wearing ancient gold rings it is said that some of the villagers received gold coins from their priest. The priest's spending spree only added weight to the rumours that he had found a great treasure.

The problems most commentators have with the story are well known. They are based on the assumption that Henry Lincoln's geometric design superimposed on the painting is correct, and secondly, that the Codes and Ciphers associated with the parchments and head stone play a critical role in the solution of the mystery. Without substantive new evidence it would be difficult to extricate oneself from these constraints and find a new direction from which to make a fresh start. I reluctantly put Lincoln's book to one side considering that there was little point in pursuing a lost cause.

A few days later, unable to set my mind free of the *Accursed Treasure,* with the book once again to hand and a renewed determination to make sense of the mystery, I began the process of making odd notes and thinking of lines and the structure of the painting. Almost without noticing what I was doing I found myself placing the straight edge my notepaper over the heads of the second and third shepherds and their female companion. I was intrigued to discover all three heads were in a straight line. Of course one could not rule out the possibility of a coincidence, nonetheless it prompted me to take a closer look at the casual group of people around an ancient tomb.

A Sketch of
Poussin's Painting ... 'Les Bergers d'Arcadie'

Figure 2-2

The *gazes and gestures* of the characters in the painting were noticeably directional. The first shepherd on the left, who I will refer to as Shepherd 'A', is leaning nonchalantly against the tomb with his outstretched left arm appearing to point towards the third Shepherd 'C', whilst at the same time gazing down at Shepherd 'B'. This shepherd although pointing to the shadow on the tomb is also directing ones attention to the tall female, while Shepherd 'C' is looking into the distance.

Imaginary lines were revealing themselves on the painting and the outline closely resembled the symbol, which I refer to as a *triangle with tails* that is on Parchment One. With a few strokes of the pen that symbol was easily drawn through the heads of the shepherds. It was also seen that whereas the *upper tail* of the symbol might terminate with the head of the female the *lower tail* went beyond Shepherd 'C' and was open ended.

This approach to the problem was not something I had come across in other literature on the subject; it seemed too easy to spot and must have occurred to others. Nevertheless, as a starting point it looked hopeful and it was time to take a closer look at the painting.

Chapter 3
Les Berger's d'Arcadie

Nicolas Poussin was born at Les Andelys in Normandy in 1594 and died in Rome in 1665. As a young man he had made his way to Paris to study. He left his native France in 1624 and journeyed to Rome where he became acquainted with the important Barberini family headed by Pope Urban V111. In 1630 he married Anne-Marie Dughet in the Church of San Lorenzo in Lucina where his remains are now interred. For a period of two years, around 1640, he returned to France to the Court of King Louis X1V of France, but left at the earliest opportunity and returned to Italy.

Figure 3-1

The monument to the painter at San Lorenzo was erected two hundred years after his death and depicts a carved bas-relief of 'Les Berger's d'Arcadie', chosen by Louis Deprez and incorporated in a design by De Chateaubriand. Underneath that picture is an inscription, probably added as an afterthought, (here translated from the Latin) - *'Refrain from pious tears, for Poussin in the Urn lives on, who yielded himself to death, unknown. Here, although he is silent, if you wish to hear him speak, the wonder is he lives and speaks in his pictures'.*

Under the circumstances it is unlikely the design by Deprez was a coincidence, but just how much of the affair he knew or who commissioned him is unknown. The later Latin inscription raises the question, how far down the line from the Cardinals or Poussin did knowledge of the treasure extend, for someone clearly had an interest in preserving the secret. The date of the monument brings us close to the time twenty-five years later when Sauniere uncovered the treasure. The two events might in some way be related if the priest of St. Mary Magdalene had visited Rome on a pilgrimage and seen the painter's memorial. The painting is not the most important of Poussin's work, but the fact that it is set in stone in relief form on his monument together with an obvious message to read his paintings would not have gone unnoticed, particularly as the very tomb depicted in the painting was within a *stones throw* from where Sauniere lived.

This painting, which is here referred to as the *Louvre*, is a well-crafted painting that at its current market value is worth a King's ransom; its potential value being worth his throne. Louis X1V of France would have given much to know its secret. After it left the King's collection it became very popular with other painters, poets and writers of the day when it was admired for its artistic eloquence. Today it is more readily associated with the *Treasure of Rennes-le-Chateau*. There is an earlier version of the 'Arcadian Shepherds', known as the *Chatsworth,* which was painted around 1627.

The modern Art World does not share the King's Louis X1V belief that this or any of Poussin's paintings contain reference to treasure, which Henry Lincoln was to discover. He sought the opinion of Anthony Blunt the one time surveyor of the Queen's pictures. Blunt rejected Lincoln's evidence as mere coincidence and refused to acknowledge that Poussin was ever in that part of France around Arques. The tomb in the painting, as well as the landscape was considered imaginary.

None the less, the Tomb of Arques did exist and the remains of the base may still be seen at Pontils on the road to Arques, where Poussin had it constructed. Blunt was a leading expert in the art world and having dismissed Lincoln's representations it is now unlikely other experts would risk their reputation and concede there were similarities within the picture and the scene at Pontils. The earlier *Chatsworth*, now in the Duke of Devonshire collection at Chatsworth House, formed part of the inventory of Cardinal Camillo Massimi who was a contemporary of Cardinal Francesco Barberini. The Barberini had commissioned the *Chatsworth* of Poussin eight or nine years after the Bolognese painter Guercino's work of 1618 failed to fulfil expectations. Poussin had proved himself a fine artist and someone who could be trusted following commissions from the Barberini family. Most notable among his work was the painting, *The Death of Germanicus* that was completed in 1627, the same year as the *Chatsworth.*

A bond of trust developed between the Holy man and the painter. It enabled them to work together in a harmony that endured for many years and which was eventually to include Cardinal Massimi. Poussin realised early in the relationship that his commission went far beyond the normality of producing a work of art. He was in possession of information, which as the Abbe Fouquet wrote to his brother, of things ... *'which even kings would have great difficulty in drawing from him* (Poussin)'. The painter was also aware that the treasures were no more accessible to him than for the Cardinals. The challenge was immense and Poussin proved he was the man for the occasion. The *Louvre* was to have been completed at the same time as the *Chatsworth* painting and to be part of a portfolio; other pictures were intended to have a supporting role.

This work will demonstrate that without the copy of the *Louvre* painting Sauniere could not have discovered the treasure. This much is clear, for he used the alignment of the three hills and the painting's link with the symbol on Parchment One. Although in the initial stages it was an *Act of God* that helped Sauniere along the way it was the trail in the picture, which he followed and that eventually led him to the treasure.

In the Art world the *Louvre* is viewed as being *quiet, but monumental.* It is said to give us *food for thought* and remind us that *even in the midst of idyllic life there is death.* The earlier dreamy setting of its counterpart the *Chatsworth* is replaced in the *Louvre* with a note of melancholy, grave and solemn that has taken on its own air of mystery. The challenge is to explore its depths and unveil the secrecy that surrounds it. Henry Lincoln's superimposing of a pentagon on the painting does not work. The idea may have looked good and has been developed, but the painting was then set aside. In describing the symbol on Parchment One as a *triangle with tails* I am not ignoring the letter 'm' above it and the figure '1' within the triangle. There is nothing lost by looking at the symbol in a different way. For instance, it was noted that when the 'm' is turned on its side it resembles the figure '3'. Set out in this way we can employ the simple mathematical sum of adding the '3' and the '1' making '4' in total; admittedly not the most astute observation, but there are four figures around the tomb, three shepherds and one female.

Lincoln's attempt at drawing pentagonal lines on the painting is not a satisfactory solution and does not equate with the lines of the symbol on Parchment One, which are easily superimposed on the painting over the heads of the shepherds. It was worth taking a closer look at the characters around the tomb.

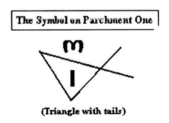

The Symbol on Parchment One

(Triangle with tails)

Figure 3-2

Poussin's characters are intent on something of interest on the tomb, but it was the direction of their focus and gestures that attracted my attention.

Imaginary lines had appeared as if by magic to mimic the shape of the icon on Parchment One. To prove there is no mistake is simplicity itself ... ANYONE may verify these findings. This simple exercise was either to prove of no practical value, or it would take me along a path hitherto unexplored and result in an amazing discovery. A closer look at the figures confirms the gestures are quite pointed; the shepherd on the left, leaning nonchalantly on the tomb, is looking down at his kneeling companion, whilst his arm is lying along the line of the lower 'tail' in the symbol.

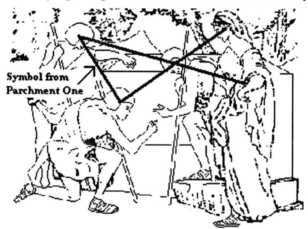

Symbol from Parchment One

The 'Triangle with tails' sits over the heads
of the Shepherds.

Figure 3-3

The kneeling shepherd is not only pointing at the inscription on the tomb but is indicating an upward direction. The head of the third shepherd intersects the lines of the upper and lower 'tails' and confirms the triangle. He is also pointing back at the second shepherd whilst gazing into the distance; the tall female companion represents the end of the upper tail and is looking down the line. ... This is no coincidence; there is a correlation between the symbol on Parchment One and the imaginary lines through the heads of the shepherds and is confirmation of a link between the painting and the documents discovered in the church of Mary Magdalene at Rennes-le-Chateau.

Sauniere may not have immediately recognised the connection, but it is clear in his pictures of the Stations of the Cross that he did understand the implications. Poussin had no intention of making the treasure easy to find and the priest was hard-pressed to work out his next step. The Holy man of Rennes experienced frustrating and anxious times; he was so close and yet so often foiled. Today's commentators on the treasure have no less information on the subject than Sauniere; he found the treasure with what was to hand ... and so might we.

CHAPTER 4
REVELATIONS IN THE PAINTING

Berenger Sauniere saw that there was more to Poussin's painting than demonstrating that the symbol on Parchment One could be superimposed over the heads of the shepherds. At the time the priest took the documents to his Bishop I suspect he had identified Poussin as the author of the parchments, although it may be misplaced conjecture on my part to suggest that Sauniere had visited Rome, seen Poussin's memorial and made the connection between the picture and the Tomb of Arques. If he had visited the City, as there is no record of Sauniere having visited the Louvre, it is possible he acquired the paintings when in Rome. Whatever the facts of the case it is clear the priest recognised the essential role of the painting and that the parchments alone did not solve the mystery.

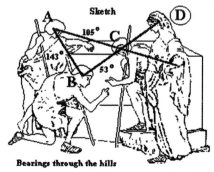

Figure 4-1

In the painting I have identified the characters around the tomb in alphabetical order, in a left to right sequence with the *nonchalant* shepherd as shepherd 'A'. At first it was thought that shepherd 'B' was pointing at the shadow on the side of the tomb but closer scrutiny reveals he is singling out the letter 'R' in the word 'ARCADIA', with Shepherd 'C' appearing to be saying, *'look what my companion is pointing at'*. In the word Arcadia, after the *highlighted* letter 'R' comes the letter 'C'. This (aRCadia) should immediately attract attention offering the possibility that we have a reference to Rennes (le) Chateau. Admittedly this was a chance discovery and something Sauniere did not see straightaway; commentators on the painting and treasure seekers have certainly overlooked it.

Sauniere's village is on a prominent hill and it occurred to me that the shepherds in the painting might represent hills. Within the vicinity of Rennes-le-Chateau there is one hill that dominates everything else around; it is Cardou. At its peak there is a blaze of chalky white outcrop … very distinctive. In fact, just as the white headdress on the tall female in Poussin's painting.

**The Shepherds Pointing Fingers
in Poussin's Painting**

Figure 4-2

Inside the cover of Henry Lincoln's book is a small-scale map of the area around Rennes-le-Chateau. If Poussin was using the heads of the shepherds to represent salient features such as hills, it should be possible to identify them. Starting with Cardou and Rennes-le-Chateau it was, following the pattern of the symbol, fairly easy to find other hills that looked promising; they were Auriol and Bois du Lauzet.

With the aid of Lincoln's reproduction of Poussin's painting and a schoolboy's protractor the approximate angles made by the lines through the heads of the shepherds were measured and compared with guidelines drawn through the hills on the map. This confirmed the pattern, but also revealed the three-dimensional effect Poussin had built into the picture. If the tall female on the right of the picture represented the 795 metre high hill Cardou, the heights of the other shepherd's heads might correspond with the lower hills in the vicinity.

Moving in a southwesterly direction from Cardou we find that Auriol has a height of 545 metres, Bois du Lauzet is at 503 metres high, with

Rennes-le-Chateau at around 600 metres above sea level. The correlation between the head heights of the shepherds and the hills was remarkable and in my opinion leaving no doubt over the authenticity of the Parchment and their association with the painting.

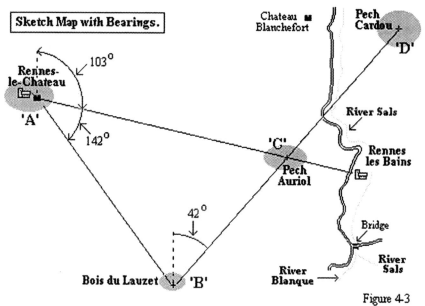

Figure 4-3

Henry Lincoln has demonstrated that within the Parchment text he discovered the message, *'This treasure belongs to Dagobert 11 King and to Sion and he is there dead'*, and, *'The treasure of Rennes-le-Chateau is only for the priesthood'*. Having concluded that both the Parchments and the painting are by Poussin and that the characters in the picture represented the nearby hills, I was convinced the painting was in fact a treasure map.

The approximate bearings through the imaginary lines on the painting were recorded as: from Shepherd 'A' to Shepherd 'B' being 143°; from 'B' through 'C' to the Female the bearing is 53° and from 'A' through Shepherd 'C' it is 105°. Although the map is a small-scale reproduction an approximation was sufficient to confirm I was on the right track. - The official map for the area is Quillan 2347 OT at a scale of 1:25000. The same notation for the heads of the shepherds, in the painting is used on the map in Figure 4-3.

When the crude bearings were checked against the official map, the angles or bearings were, from shepherd 'A' to shepherd 'B', 142 degrees. From shepherd 'B' through 'C' to the female 'D' the bearing is 42 degrees and from shepherd 'A', following the line of his arm, the bearing to 'C' is 103 degrees. On the larger scale map the high point of the respective hills can be more accurately determined and the revised bearings are illustrated. The difference is just one degree from 'A' through to 'B', two degrees from 'A' through 'C' and about ten degrees difference (53 to 42) from 'B' to 'D'. Apart from the first two bearings the angle made by line 'BD' is the only notable variation. This makes no difference to the outcome and is considered to be within *Artist's licence.*

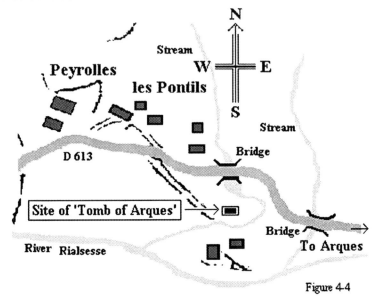

Figure 4-4

The realisation that here at last, step-by-step, the path to the treasure was being traced was quite overwhelming. However that was not all, there were more revelations to be brought to light from the painting.

Figure 4-5

For two hundred and fifty years until 1988 the old tomb, which closely resembles the one in Poussin's painting, had stood on the rocky promontory across the gorge from the present bridge at Pontils on the Road to Arques. Henry Lincoln has a photograph of it in his book; sadly today only the base remains. The painter had carefully chosen the location and had the edifice constructed. When one stands on the bridge at Pontils looking across at the site of the tomb, one is facing south, with the shadow of the head of Shepherd 'B' on the tomb, *suggesting* the time of day might be before noon. … The painter Abraham Bruegel once asked Poussin how he had attained the mastery that had granted him such an exalted place among the great painters of Italy. Poussin modestly answered, "I neglect nothing". … Poussin was meticulous in all he did and as every trained artist he undoubtedly understood the effects of light, shade and shadow.

From the beginning of time the Sun has cast its shadow and in Poussin's day it was no different. In the northern hemisphere, had the tomb still been in place, a shadow cast by the Sun would not have fallen on the north side of the edifice which we would see from the road and as is depicted in the painting.

It was not a simple error or oversight on Poussin's part, it was quite deliberate, the painter knew exactly what he was doing. He could not have made the message clearer if he had written it across the top of the picture. The shadow of shepherd B's finger, *even if the Sun was in the Northern Hemisphere*, should be 'touching' the knee of shepherd 'C', whereas it is with its finger on the shadow of the head, together with shepherd 'C's finger. The shadow is used to make an amazing statement … it's the *head*, the *head*, the *head*! … The heads are the intersection points for the three lines of the triangle in the symbol and the staffs the shepherds are holding are 'lines', the sides of the triangle.

Plate - 1

Plate 2

27

CHAPTER 5
THE PARCHMENTS

Those who have visited Rennes-le-Chateau and the little church of St Mary Magdalene might imagine the moment after the storm when the priest stared in disbelief at the damage around him and the shock of seeing his Communion Table in a state of collapse.

His first reaction was to seek help but something restrained his impulse to rush out of the church and instead he calmly set about collecting the scattered Altarpieces before contemplating the task of rebuilding his table. It was as he struggled to lift the heavy slab that he saw one of the fallen pillars had been hollowed out and contained a wooden tube, which he withdrew and put to one side. It was later in the day that the priest opened the container and discovered the Parchments.

All that remains of the original Altar is the short length of hollowed out pillar, which was first used by Sauniere as a plinth to the statue of the Virgin in the grounds of the church; it is now inverted and forms part of the Presbytery Museum exhibition. The wooden tube has long since gone and all we are left with is what purports to be facsimiles of the original parchments. The Altar had stood undisturbed for 240 years and had the course of history turned out differently, might be there to this day.

On that day in the late 1630's as the painter Nicolas Poussin dropped the wooden tube into the Altar pillar, just before the masons set the heavy

Communion Slab on the pillars, he could not have imagined that an act of God and an astute minor priest would upset his carefully laid plans.

As the Abbe Louis Fouquet later reported, Poussin confidently expected that - *it is possible that nobody else will ever rediscover (his secret) in the centuries to come* - It was a secret that the Cardinals had entrusted to Poussin and which was to have been sealed forever, known *only to the priesthood* of the day. The painter must have realised that confiding in Abbe Fouquet knowledge of the existence of an immense treasure would sow the seeds of intrigue and the possibility of the secret being discovered.

In his book Henry Lincoln's has reproductions of the two Parchments, authenticity of which is disputed. The documents are considered by some to be modern-day fakes. But as Lincoln says, *it mattered not the slightest if the parchments were old, fake or modern; they were confusing* – which may be so, but more than that, the fact remains that what we see reproduced in current literature is all we have and it is these documents that will be examined in detail.

Figure 5-1

It will be assumed that before taking the documents to Paris for verification Sauniere had them copied and it is these copies, which were later to be discovered among the papers he left with Marie Denarnaud.

Although the priest experienced difficulty in finding the treasure he did so with the information we have today and it will be shown that the Parchments predate Sauniere and are not modern-day fakes. The drawings, such as Figure 5.1, are sketches of reproductions found in a number of books on the subject of the treasure.

Within the text of the Parchment, referred to as Parchment One, we find at the beginning of the top line of the Parchment the letters 'ET', and at the end of that line the letters, 'IN'; recognisable as the first two words in, 'Et In Arcadia Ego' and associated with the painting *Les Berger's d'Arcadie*.

Henry Lincoln was introduced to King Dagobert 11's treasure when he picked up a book by Gerard de Sède entitled, Le Tresor Maudit ('The Accursed Treasure'). His fixation with the story was probably the catalyst that set a whole industry in search of the *Treasure of Rennes-le-Chateau*. Almost all authors on the subject base their narrative on the guiding principles laid down by Lincoln, though they interpret the source of the priest's wealth in different ways. Lincoln found that within the text of Parchment One there were letters raised out of line from which a code could be created. His expert observation led to, ... *'This treasure belongs to Dagobert 11 King and to Sion and he is there dead'*.

Lincoln then went on to construct a triangle as an overlay based on the letters and the symbols in the parchment. In lines 4, 7 and 10 of Parchment One there are, instead of letters, plus marks, '+' that are highlighted on the sketch within the small triangles. He commences his main triangle in extending the 'lower tail' of the top symbol by drawing a line, (my notation) from 'A' to the first '+' at 'B' in line 4. From there his second line passes through an, 'S', an 'I', and 'O' and the '+' in line 10 to terminate with the letter 'N' at 'C'in the last line. Lincoln then completes his basic triangle ABC by drawing the third line from the 'N' up through the side of the symbol to 'A'. On the face of it this exercise seems reasonable as Lincoln's line 'BC' passes through a cross, the letters 'S', 'I', 'O', (another cross) and an N to spell out the word SION ... Jerusalem and the Temple. Unfortunately, from his basic triangle, the author then leads us into an area of geometric designs resulting in the possibilities of, *astrological and alchemical signs for the Sun and Moon and five-pointed star,* based on a geometric structure on the painting. Those who study the construction of paintings may readily understand Lincoln's approach and the advice he was given.

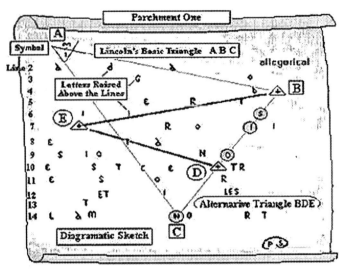

Figure 5-2

In Parchment One Henry Lincoln draws the conclusion that the clear text is a compound of Gospel versions of the story, which tells of Jesus and the Disciples walking in the cornfields on the Sabbath day. The Scriptural references may be seen in Matthew chapter 12, verses 1 to 4 (4 verses); Mark chapter 2, verses 23 to 26 (4 verses) and in Luke chapter 6 verses 1 to 4 (again 4 verses). If the three Gospels are represented in the text then the crosses '+' on the Parchment may indicate the division of the verses. … Three crosses equal four blocks of verses. *"Although the text is clear there is the instantly obvious oddity of the lines being arranged in a curious fashion, ending sometimes in the middle of a word"* (Lincoln).

All the verses tell of Jesus and the disciples eating corn from the cornfields on the Sabbath and of how King David went into the Temple and ate the showbread. Poussin seems to be drawing attention to Jesus (St. Nazaire). The *Corn* signifies *treasure* and *Temple,* the *church.* The crosses on line 4, lines 7 and line 10 not only divide groups of verses but also would serve as triangle intersection points.

It is also worth mentioning that the same crosses are to be found on the so-called Grave Slab, which will be examined later. On that slab, in the left-hand column of Latin and Greek letters we read ... ET IN A + PX ... in the right hand column we find A Δ (Delta) + I A E r Ω (Omega); the crosses '+' separate groups of letters.

My Diagrammatic Sketch of Parchment One shows Lincoln's triangle Lines ABC using only one cross as an intersection point. The 'Alternative Triangle' B D E engages the three crosses, but the resulting geometric figure does not match the Parchment Symbol, although the line 'ED' might assume the bearing Rennes-le-Chateau to Rennes les Bains and the line 'DB' is Auriol to Cardou. Stanley James in his book, *The Treasure Maps of Rennes-le-Chateau* uses the crosses in much the same way and comes close to solving the meaning of the symbol on Parchment One. At the bottom of the Parchment we have another symbol in the form of a 'P' and 'S' contained within a partial loop (P-S). An almost identical symbol is to be found on the Grave Slab. By taking the preceding alphabetical letters in the symbol, Lincoln has suggested it signifies the French word, OR, for Gold.

Both Parchments appear to be by the same hand and although there seems little evidence on which to claim that Nicolas Poussin wrote the Parchments that is by no means all. Poussin did not always sign his works and when he did his signature is not consistent. In the painting *The Martyrdom of Erasmus,* he signed it 'Nicolaus Pusin'. In our particular case his *signature* on Parchment Two is amazingly clever, very revealing with a dual role that will be seen to provide an indispensable aid in seeking the treasure. The painter was commissioned to record a secret that had been passed down by word of mouth and which was becoming burdensome to those who held it. It was not something to be entrusted to anyone; an earlier attempt employing the painter Guercino proved unsatisfactory. It required a talented man with considerable imagination. Subsequent evidence shows that the painter's ingenuity knew no bounds; it was astounding, involving the *Altar* at Mary Magdalene, the *Parchments, Grave Slab, Tomb of Arques* and the paintings.

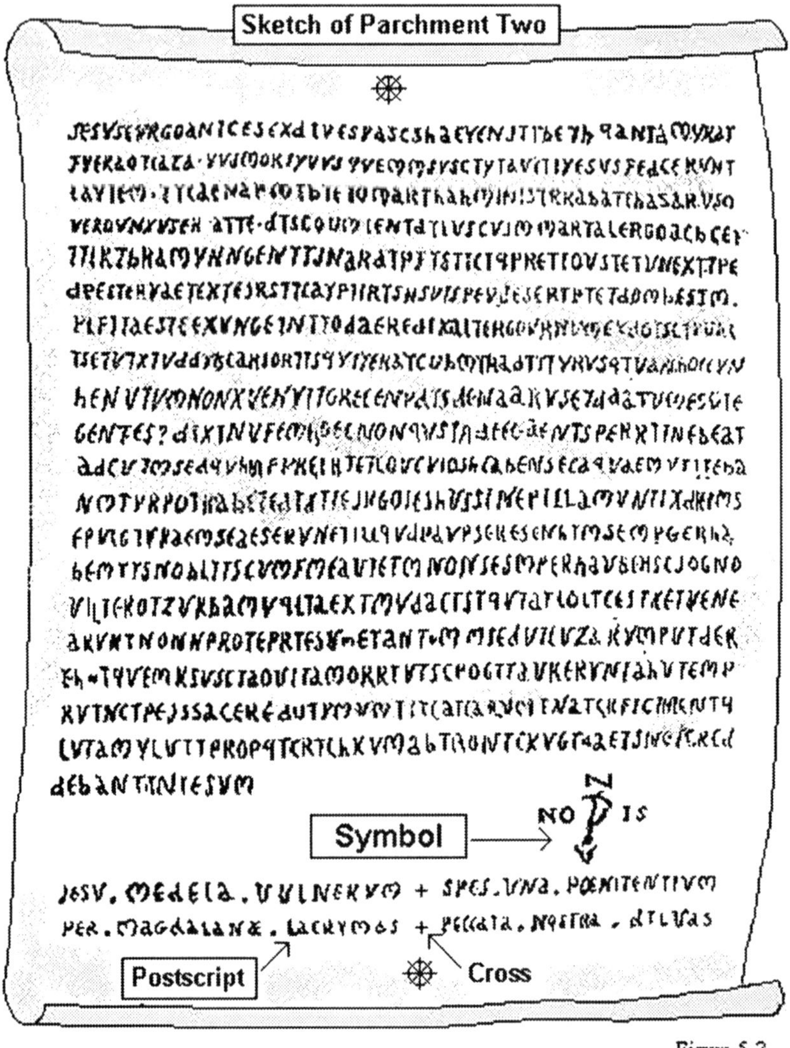

Figure 5-3

All this was designed that the secret should never be lost to those who were. *Only of the priesthood* and could read the signs.

In Parchment Two the bulk of the text relates a story found in John's Gospel chapter 12 verses 1 to 11 inclusive.

"Then Jesus, six days before the Passover came to Bethany where Lazarus had been raised from the dead. There they made Him a supper; and Martha served: and Lazarus sat at the table with him. Then Mary took a pound of ointment of spikenard, very costly, and anointed the feet of Jesus, and wiped his feet with her hair: and the house was filled with the odour of the ointment. Then the disciple Judas Iscariot, who would

betray Him asked why was not this ointment sold for three hundred pence and given to the poor. Then Jesus said, let her alone: against the day of my burying hath she kept this. For the poor always ye have with you, but me ye have not always. Many people of the Jews therefore knew that He was there: and they came not for Jesus' sake only, but that they might see Lazarus also. But the chief priests consulted that they might put Lazarus also to death. Because that by reason of him many of the Jews went away and believed on Jesus'.

The reason for Poussin choosing part of John's Gospel is not entirely clear as some of the additional letters appear to serve no useful purpose. If the painter felt he was making the solution of the puzzle too easy and built in a *red herring,* his ploy worked. Many people have spent time and energy trying to resolve the *Codes and ciphers,* based on those additional letters.

Following the Scripture verses of the text, but within the same chapter, the raising of Lazarus from the dead is described. In that text we find ...
... *"Jesus went to Bethany (the house of dates), a village near Jerusalem, the home of Lazarus and his sisters Martha and Mary".* – Sauniere's villa is named Bethanie, ... In Verse 38 we read, *'Jesus cometh to the grave'.* - It was a cave, and a stone lay upon it'. In the frontispiece picture to his church Altar Sauniere shows a cave with a 'stone' in the form of a skull at its entrance.

Henry Lincoln has shown that the text on Parchment Two contains hidden messages that he has read as, 'To Genesareth' (Lake Genesareth or the Sea of Galilee) - And, 'Bread and Salt'. The first part I have taken to mean, *to the water,* and the second as a direct reference to the rivers Blanque and the Sals at Rennes les Bains.

The description of Mary anointing the feet of Jesus is interesting. That which is at the feet of Jesus is very valuable ... Indeed it is.

Jesus, the Church - at the foot of the Church - Below the Church.

Henry Lincoln has also concluded ... *'The Corn* (money) *of Redis* (is) *only for the priesthood'*, or, *'The Treasure of Rennes-le-Chateau* is only for the initiated', for the clergy ... Unmistakably a Church connection.

Almost without exception every Artist signs his or her work. Every document or letter we receive or write bears a signature, or an identifying mark indicating its originator. Rarely, but sometimes an identifying mark may be in the form of a monogram, comprising two or more letters combined in a design. On Parchment Two the symbol towards the bottom of the scroll has a dual role, it is both a Symbol and a Monogram, below which we have a postscript.

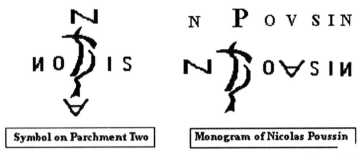

| Symbol on Parchment Two | Monogram of Nicolas Poussin |

Figure 5-4

When the symbol was examined it was noted that at its centre was a crude letter 'P'. At the top is the letter 'N' whilst at the bottom is an inverted 'A'. We also have an, 'O', 'S', 'I', and another 'N'. The combination of these letters may be contrived to give us a name ... N Povsin. ... It is a monogram, a signature and it is the signature of the painter Nicolas Poussin. Below the main block of text and the symbol we read: -

'Jesu Medeia uvinekum + spes una poenitentium
per Magdalane lackymas + peccata nostka diluas'

This is interpreted as, -

'Jesus healer of wounds the one hope of repentance through the tears of Magdalene wash away our sins'. 'Jesus is the Church, Rennes les Bains is the Bathing place' and the 'Tears of Magdalene' are the Rivers Blanque and Sals.

The Parchments, far from being fakes or a modern-day hoax prove to be good facsimiles of the original documents which the priest Berenger Sauniere discovered. The texts of the documents, when decoded reveal statements pointing to Dagobert 11 and his treasure with the symbol on the first Parchment providing the link with the painting *Les Berger's d'Arcadie.* Its' counterpart on Parchment Two holds a double meaning; on the one hand it seals the authorship of the documents and on the other it will be seen to be an intricately detailed pointer to the site of the treasure.

CHAPTER 6
MORE THAN A MONOGRAM

Berenger Sauniere had no idea of the treasure he was about to discover. He might have guessed it was more than a few gold coins after finding the Parchments and understanding the alignment of the hills in relation to the heads of the shepherds in the painting, together with the symbol on Parchment One.

The priest had noted that the *upper tail* of the symbol from Parchment One, when superimposed on the painting, closed with the head of the tall female who represented Cardou the highest hill in the immediate area. The line of the *lower tail* of the symbol was open-ended, there being no other obvious hill in the vicinity he saw it as a general directional indicator. The countryside around his village was well known to him and it would have been clear, from his vantage point on the hill that the line was heading for the Spa town of Rennes les Bains, which is in the valley east of Rennes-le-Chateau. It is also probable he had read and understood the clue, 'To (the lake) Genesareth' in the Parchment as meaning, 'To the Water'.

The Biblical Jesus of Nazareth frequented the area around Lake Genesareth or the Sea of Galilee where He performed the miracle of turning the water into wine and it is wine, which is referred to in the relief carving on the Altar pillar at St Mary Magdalene. The small spa town of Rennes les Bains is a straggling community, which follows the river Sals, noted for its bathing and hot springs since pre Roman times. It is *Royal*

Redis the place of kings and it is where we find the last resting place of King Dagobert 11 and his treasure.

From the so-called Grave slab Lincoln has deduced that the,' *The gold at Rennes is at Royal Redis in the storerooms of the fortress'*. Rennes les Bains is '*Royal Redis',* where we will find '*the storerooms of the fortress'*. A further clue to the treasure is that its location is in a place, which is, '*only for the priesthood'*. As there is no castle at Rennes the church seems a likely candidate.

The evidence was pointing ever more to the certainty of the link between the Parchments and the painting and that there was no other explanation for the meaning of the symbol on Parchment Two. It is a monogram, the signature of the painter Nicolas Poussin. Indeed, it was more than a monogram.

When we look again at the symbol we see there is a 'N' at the top and an inverted 'A' at the bottom that together resemble a directional indicator. Henry Lincoln 'flipped' the symbol about the horizontal to produce 'ZION' – a church, a place of worship and Jerusalem. It also had the effect of altering the direction of the arrow from southwest to southeast; this is not important as it depends from which unknown northern point one takes direction.

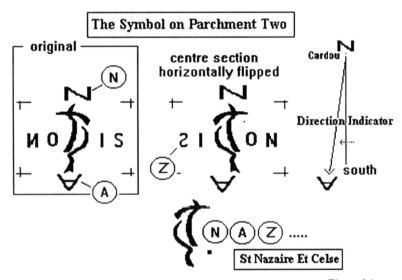

Figure 6-1

The priest reputedly brought back from Paris prints of the painting, *Les Berger's d'Arcadie* by Poussin, *St. Anthony Hermit,* by Teniers and a portrait of Pope Celestine V. The latter was not considered of interest, but the Teniers picture was thought to be important, mainly because of the inverted 'A' in the symbol and the possibility of the church being dedicated to St Anthony. Unfortunately there was no information that would confirm to whom the church at Rennes les Bains was dedicated. A way around the problem was required and subsequent enquiries resulted in a surprising outcome, one that was not at first understood. It was Michele who contacted the Syndicat d'initiatives Musee archeologique at Rennes les Bains and came back with the news that the church in that place was dedicated to St Nazaire Et Celse. This news changed the course of my thinking and deepened the mystery. The mystery was partially solved by Henry Lincoln's reversal of the Parchment Two symbol, for in doing so the crude 'P' at the centre of the symbol took on a completely different form and meaning. Instead of the *letter* being taken as a 'P', it was easily broken down into two separate letters, a 's' and a 't'. This gives us the 'st', as in Saint. In its original form both the 'N' and 'S' in SION are reversed, but when flipped give the true letters of 'Z' and 'N'. The arrowhead remains inverted, but provides the letter 'A' and as the drawing demonstrates, we then have the 'st', the 'N', 'A' and 'Z'. ... It was not difficult to complete the remaining letters of the clue to uncover the name of the place where the treasure can be located.

Poussin had been clever and there was no mistaking the clue. ... Dagobert's gold, or the *Treasure of Rennes-le-Chateau* is in the 'fortress', the Church *of St. Nazaire Et Celse*, in Rennes les Bains. The symbol was *more than a monogram* confirming that it was Nicolas Poussin who wrote the Parchments and had concealed them in the Altar pillar in the church of St Mary Magdalene at Rennes-le-Chateau. ... If there is merit in further examination of either the Teniers or the portrait it was not immediately evident.

The Devils Armchair

Visigoth's Pillar

Apprentice's pillar

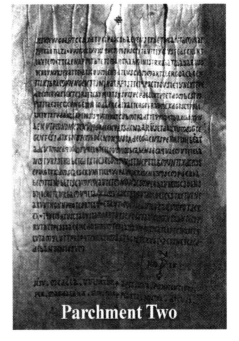

Parchment Two

Plate 3

Montsegur

Tour Magdala

Cardou

Author at
Standing Stone

Plate 4

Chapter 7
The Visigoth Pillar

    Within the vicinity of the church of Mary Magdalene there are a number of buildings and features; the Church itself, the Cemetery, the Presbytery which Sauniere restored and where he lived. The Calvary, erected in 1897, the Grotto dedicated to Mary Magdalene and at one time the Carolingian or Visigoth Pillar thought to date from the 8th or 9th century. The short length of square sectioned Altar pillar, which is now inverted in the Presbytery Museum, was once in the grounds of the church as a plinth to the statue of Mary the Virgin; a mock-up pillar now supports the statue.

**The Altar in the Church of Mary Magdalene
by Nicolas Poussin**

Figure 7-1

Although it is assumed the Altar was built during the 8th or 9th Century during the time the Visigoths occupied Reddae, the earlier name for Rennes-le-Chateau that is not the case. The Altar was designed and built by Nicolas Poussin around 1640 AD. It was that Altar which fell apart and was reset by Berenger Sauniere after the storm and from which Sauniere had retrieved the Parchments and I believe discovered the so-called *Grave Slab* as the table top. General use and fair wear and tear over two hundred years left the joints between the stone surfaces in a weakened state and the entire Altar vulnerable to dislodgement, when subjected to a severe jolt. The painter was convinced that, *'even in the centuries to come'* the secret would not be rediscovered; he was not to know that an Act of God – or a deliberate push would undo all his carefully laid plans.

When the Altar was first assembled it comprised of a plinth stone, the pillar section and a capping stone; the figures beneath the cross-headed screw suggest there were at least two pillars supporting the tabletop slab.

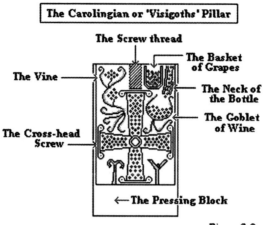

Figure 7-2

The carvings on the sides of the pillar are interwoven lattice and circles, with its face typifying the process of wine making, the industry of the region. The centrepiece of the design is the cross, which is also a cross-headed screw used to tighten a press. The thread of the screw may be seen above the cross. The vine is in the upper left portion of the stone, the basket of grapes is immediately to the right of the thread, with the goblet resting on the right hand crosspiece; the wine is pouring from the neck of a bottle above it. At the foot of the cross is a pressing block, which until Berenger Sauniere had it inscribed with, 'Mission 1891' was plain stone.

Many a person standing before that Altar would understand the carving portrayed on the pillars except for the symbols either side of the foot of the crosspiece. These symbols may have a perfectly rational explanation, other than considered here. On the left the symbol is not easily recognised until it is compared with its counterpart on the right. One of the pillars is hollow and before the heavy tabletop was lowered into position the writer of the Parchments placed the wooden container tube into the cavity, telling the workers they were his design drawings of the Altar. The mason would have nodded his approval and as time passed the incident was largely forgotten. However, in a small community where tales were passed from generation to generation the idea that there was something in one of the pillars may not have been entirely lost. Berenger Sauniere who must also have puzzled over the picture presented on the face of that pillar began to see a solution to the mystery and the damaging storm provided him with an opportunity to put his theory to the test.

MISSION
1891

And Samson took hold
of the two middle
pillars upon which the
house stood and on which
it was borne up, the one
with his right hand the
other with his left
Judges 16.29

Figure 7-3

If the two symbols are identified with the art of wine making then the face of that pillar is just a picture. But it was more than that; those peculiar little shapes were part of an elaborate clue, *"These things are so difficult to discover..."* (Poussin). The symbol on the right resembles a 'Y', two arms upraised. The right arm of the 'Y' actually touches the lower scroll on the crosspiece and each arm is topped with a 'block' … a part of a slab. The other symbol on the left appears to indicate the arms of the 'Y' are limp and hanging down.

The purpose of the symbols now becomes clear. The left hand side of the slab is not to be raised. The significance of the right hand symbol is that it requires strength; two arms up stretched. The design seems to draw on scripture and the story of Samson who stood between two pillars … Poussin is saying, *'lift the right hand side of the slab'*. Within the fork of the 'Y' is a 'blob' resembling a 'head' that seems to have a hollow centre; it looks down to its left. As Sauniere faced the broken Altar the morning after the storm it was the right hand pillar which was found to be hollowed and to contain the tube.

Nicolas Poussin had spent a deal of time and expenditure setting out the secret of the treasure. His patrons, the Cardinals of Rome, intended that the secrets should not be lost yet never rediscovered until the fullness of time. In theory it was (according to Poussin), doubtful if anyone, " ... *in the centuries to come would rediscover* [the treasure]". Unfortunately all the painter's meticulous handiwork was short-circuited by the aftermath of a violent storm and the irony is that against all the odds it was an opportune discovery by an unintended member of the priesthood, the priest of Rennes-le-Chateau that has led to the uncovering of Poussin's secret.

The inscription, 'Penitence! Penitence!' on the capping stone to the pillar is of unknown origin but probably was the work of Berenger Sauniere, just as the inscription 'Mission 1891'. In both cases the carving appears relatively fresh and the date of 1891 matches the inscription found on the porch of the church. The inscription may also refer to the word 'Poenitentium' in the postscript to Parchment Two.

The picture on the Pillar tells the parable of ... *'A householder who planted a vineyard and went into a far country after having leased the vineyard out. When the fruit was ready he sent his servants to receive the first of it; they met a hostile reception. He sent other servants who fared no better. Last of all he sent his son, saying, they will reverence my son; he they killed'* ... Jesus is further making the point in the parable that the *stone,* in this case the pillar, is *'the stone the builders rejected'.* It is a most important *stone* and indeed it is the stone, the pillar that has been overlooked. Poussin in referring to the story of the vineyard is directing us to a *far country.* It was at Cana in Galilee, by *the water,* where at the wedding Jesus turned the water into wine ... *Him they killed,* and, *He is there dead.* In that *far country* (of) Rennes les Bains is the remains of King Dagobert, his treasure and *by the water* is where we find *Jesus ...* St Nazaire.

It is reported that with great ceremony Sauniere installed the statue of *Our Lady of Lourdes* in the church grounds in June 1891 – the date is celebrated on the pillar with the inverted date, '1681' shown on the entrance porch to the church. On the base to the plinth of the old Altar pillar are the Alpha and Omega, the beginning and the end. The Altar pillar, with its symbols and concealed Parchments marked both the beginning and the end of the search for the treasure. In setting the statue in a prominent position Sauniere was not only drawing attention to *Our Lady of Lourdes.*

CHAPTER 8
ST. MARY, ST. NAZAIRE.

It is as if the churches of St Mary Magdalene and St Nazaire Et Celse were being *weighed in a balance.* The one occupies the high ground, the other the low ground. The pan of the balance of the church on the hill is empty and *found wanting, whilst* the pan of the balance of the Church in the valley is *full and running over.* They are pictured as being in either hand of the scales, one each side of the fulcrum, which is the hill Auriol.

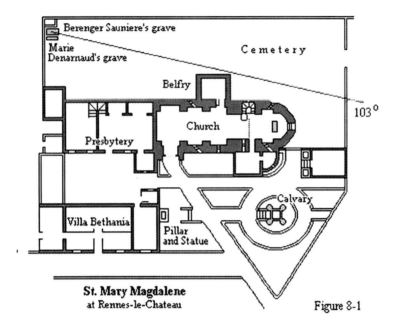

St. Mary Magdalene
at Rennes-le-Chateau

Figure 8-1

Until now the Treasure of Rennes-le-Chateau, if thought to be anywhere was within the hilltop village that bears its name, but evidence presented within these pages shows that is not the case. Neither the villager nor the visitor is walking on gold as Marie Denarnaud thought; her pastor had rightly judged her naivety and she played her part well.

The church of St. Mary Magdalene is poorly lit and shabby, not altogether unexpected for a small building receiving more than its fair share of visitors. In contrast St. Nazaire Et Celse is pleasantly bright, airy and has the ambiance and serenity of a place of worship; yet it holds a secret that is beyond belief. It truly is a *church of secrets*, a Secret Church that is the key to unimagined wealth.

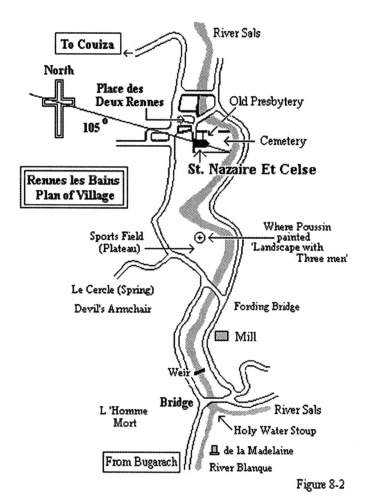

Figure 8-2

The church of Mary Magdalene at Rennes-le-Chateau underwent dramatic changes after the arrival of the parish priest Berenger Sauniere in 1885. Before that date little was known of the village and its church as only a few Diocesan notes are thought to exist.

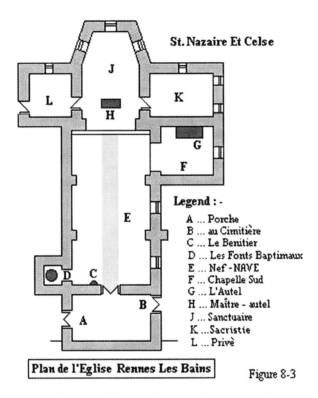

St. Nazaire Et Celse

Legend : -

A ... Porche
B ... au Cimitière
C ... Le Benitier
D ... Les Fonts Baptimaux
E ... Nef - NAVE
F ... Chapelle Sud
G ... L'Autel
H ... Maître - autel
J ... Sanctuaire
K ...Sacristie
L ... Privè

Plan de l'Eglise Rennes Les Bains   Figure 8-3

The vaults and parts of its walls are of Roman style, over which the building, as a place of worship was constructed. It was not until additions were made to the building, around 100 years later that the church was dedicated to Mary Magdalene, during the time of the Templars.

Locating the church of St. Nazaire Et Celse in Rennes les Bains is not straightforward. One must first make for the Place des Deux Rennes, then go down to the bottom right hand corner of the square, towards the salon, where there is a short alleyway leading to the church. On the left of the alleyway stands the old Presbytery where the Abbe Boudet lived for so many years and where Berenger Sauniere and Marie Denarnaud often visited. At the end of the alley there is an ornamental gateway into the entrance foyer of the church. As well as giving access to the church, the entrance allows passage through into the cemetery beyond.

The land around the church slopes down towards the boundary wall that separates the burial ground from the River Sals. From the lowest point in the cemetery one gets a good perspective of the Church with its prominent apse.

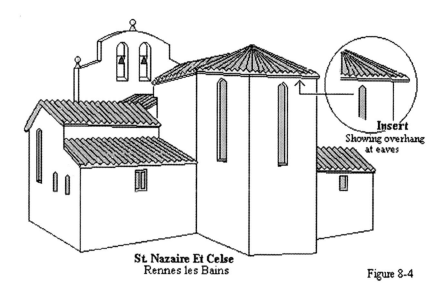

St. Nazaire Et Celse
Rennes les Bains

Figure 8-4

At first there appeared nothing obvious about the church to indicate the presence of any treasure or to raise ones expectations, but gradually as one walked around inside the building signs were noticed that increased the level of excitement. The evidence within these pages will confirm that the church of St Nazaire Et Celse is the place of Dagobert's gold and the recent *signs - some* of which may date from the time of Abbe Boudet, point to the location of the treasure having been rediscovered. The church is not well publicised, quite the opposite to Mary Magdalene. No church literature was available recording its history; indeed it was as if its very presence was to be a secret. My sketch plan is a fair representation that was produced from numerous photographs and rough dimensions.

Sauniere's unrecorded but frequent visits to Rennes-le-Bains had met with guarded acceptance by the Abbe Boudet and a workable relationship developed enabling Sauniere to share in the treasure.

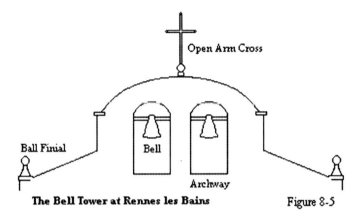

The Bell Tower at Rennes les Bains   Figure 8-5

The church of Rennes-les-Bains, which dedicated to Saint Celse and Nazaire, is an old structure probably dating from around 1162, although it is not as old as its counterpart on the hill and the clean octagonal lines of the apse, rather than the semi-circular shape of other small churches in the area, including St Mary Magdalene, give it a modern appearance.

Henri Boudet was considered a mysterious priest who served at Rennes les-Bains for 42 years and like Sauniere spent large sums of money indulging him in a comfortable lifestyle as well as being a generous benefactor to the needy of his parish.

It is almost certain that Boudet had early in his ministry discovered the treasure, something that Sauniere came to realise after decoding the Parchments at Mary Magdalene and had it not been for the younger man's greed their relationship would have lasted many more years than it did. The stress of the relationship after Sauniere had offered the item to Rome did neither man's health any good and led to the untimely death of the priest of Rennes-le-Chateau.

The falling out between Boudet and Sauniere effectively ended the latter's access to Dagobert' hoard and most likely the older man's failing health probably meant that thereafter Boudet did not again visit the treasure. It may have been the case that once Sauniere was introduced to the treasure Boudet did not go back down into the cave, leaving the younger and fit man to wander at will amongst the gold. When the parting of the ways came the understanding over the treasure ceased and as neither could afford to divulge the secret it remained a closed matter between them.

Boudet had discovered Dagobert's treasure quite by chance and would have had no knowledge of the Parchments and Poussin's involvement. Nor like Sauniere, would he have had need of or be a party to the much later fabricated Codes and Ciphers, which are a bane to all modern writers interested in the Treasure of Rennes-le-Chateau.

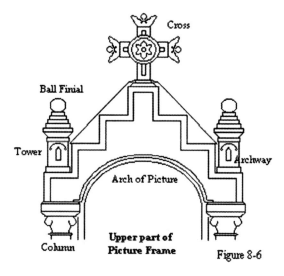

Figure 8-6

As the years passed Boudet's health and physical handicap became an increasing problem for the Bishop that he was obliged to address, and in 1914 the old priest was relieved of his post and replaced by the Abbe Rescanieres. The new priest was barely at St. Nazaire six months when he met an untimely and tragic death. As in the case of the Abbe Gelis, the mystery of Rescaniere's death was never resolved. If Sauniere was responsible for the deaths it is difficult to conclude it was other than for the surety of the treasure.

Sauniere could not have acquired the wealth he did without Boudet's involvement, but whereas Boudet's route to the treasure was no more difficult than opening a suspicious looking door, Sauniere laboriously followed the clues that Poussin had laid down. The moment must have come when Sauniere confronted Boudet and advised him of his suspicion regarding the treasure and the source of the older man's excessive wealth. From then on they both had accesses to a huge fortune.

Neither Poussin nor his patrons the Cardinals in Rome give the impression they knew precisely how to get at the treasure in St Nazaire. It was sufficient for their purposes to know where it was and consider it safe. It was Sauniere who took it upon himself to demonstrate in his pictures in the Stations of the Cross at Mary Magdalene how to gain access to the treasure. The hoard he rediscovered along with Boudet include something more important than gold and it is clear that whatever the item was neither Rome or the Holy Roman Emperors were aware it existed. The item was considered important enough to *do a deal* with Sauniere and Rome parted with a large amount of cash. Sauniere may have gambled that the rift between himself and Boudet could be healed and that he would then be able to *honour the contract*. Today the Church of Rome, that is to say the Bishop of Carcassonne, denies there is or ever was a treasure.

The priest and the painter show the link between the two churches. Poussin used classical pictures and a monument in stone whilst Sauniere leaves us gaudy plasters and paints. The painter worked on the problem under the direction of the Cardinals for years and spread the clues *far and wide*. Sauniere on the other hand placed all his eggs in one basket and although careful in his planning used *language* the locals and particularly his brother priests could recognise. The Abbe Boudet had been fairly discreet about his wealth but Sauniere made no secret of his. His sudden possession of riches set him apart from his contemporaries and probably led to a consortium against him. The inauguration day at the Church at Rennes-le-Chateau in June 1897 was the highlight of the ecclesiastical year, with the Bishop and other notable persons, including the Abbe Gelis the priest of Coustaussa in attendance. Gelis was quick to spot a weak link in Sauniere's colourful charade, and one suspects, exploited it. We can only guess at the possible consequences, but within four months of that day in June the Abbe Gelis was murdered in his presbytery. A considerable quantity of cash in the house was left untouched. Gelis had not needed to know precisely how to get to the treasure, it was sufficient for him to recognise the clue to Sauniere's wealth and threaten to reveal the source, unless suitably rewarded.

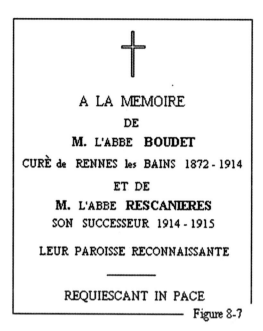

✝

A LA MEMOIRE
DE
M. L'ABBE BOUDET
CURÈ de RENNES les BAINS 1872 - 1914
ET DE
M. L'ABBE RESCANIERES
SON SUCCESSEUR 1914 - 1915

LEUR PAROISSE RECONNAISSANTE

———————

REQUIESCANT IN PACE

Figure 8-7

Although nothing was ever proven suspicions were aroused and must have served as a warning to anyone who thought they knew where Sauniere's treasure lay. A number of years after the passing of Berenger Sauniere and Boudet the location of the treasure was rediscovered, although it is unknown if the object paid for by Rome was retrieved.

After leaving the Church of St. Nazaire Et Celse on my first visit to Rennes les Bains I called at the Salon near the old Presbytery at the bottom of the Place des Deux Rennes and obtained from Madam the Abbe's address. Once back in England a short letter requesting a layout and details of the church was drafted to the Monsieur. A few weeks later a letter arrived from the church administrator with the enclosure of a pamphlet; in French of course, which unfortunately did not provide the information hoped for. Rough notes and sketches made at the time of the visit would have to do; it resulted in the sketch layout plan of the church.

A decision was made to write to the Bishop of Carcassonne, putting it to him that it was suspected the treasure was hidden within church property and seeking his advice as to procedure should it be proven. The response was prompt and not altogether surprising in its content. It looked as though the door was politely closed in ones face and it was felt better not to distress the situation with a further letter at that stage.

A translated text of the letter from the Bishop is set out below: -

From Monseigneur Jacques Despierre, Bishop of Carcassonne … it was dated 30/11/1996.

My Lord Bishop has requested me to reply to your letter, not out of disrespect to you and your request but because he thinks that I am best placed to advise you in your "premonition or inspiration", regarding the search for the Treasure of Rennes-le-Chateau. Indeed as well as being Secretary to the Bishopric, I am at the same time a member of the clergy of the Upper Aude Valley responsible for the parish of Rennes-le-Chateau.

I have confessed to you that we do not believe in the existence of the "Treasure" and that we side absolutely with the conclusions of two authoritative works, which I attach for you. These are by the Abbe Bruno de Monts and Mt Rene Descadaellas. In fact on the one hand the little story of this priest doesn't fit in with the discovery of an immense historic treasure. On the other hand the material damage, especially the moral damage is not worth the trouble of pursuing this wild figment of the imagination. The population and the Christian community of our pastoral areas have had more than enough of being the object of curiosity and tall story telling of the whole World. Therefore if you wish to continue to be interested in our department of the Aude and in the history of the Diocese of Carcassonne, both of which have authentic "archaeological Treasure" we shall remain perfectly good friends. I will also say that our sole and true richness is our Languedoc culture, our activities of yesterday and today.

With friendly greetings.

Yours sincerely, Abbe Dominique Verge.

The following Notes were attached: -

Authoritative Notes on the search for the "Treasure" of Rennes-le-Chateau.

1 / - Berenger Sauniere - vicar at Rennes-le-Chateau 1885 - 1909.

… Abbe Bruno de Monts - Edition Belisane Nice 1989.

Conclusion - L'Abbe Sauniere et le Tresor de Rennes-le-Chateau.

If there was a "Treasure" at Rennes-le-Chateau: Where and when.

In 1887 and in 1897 large bills were paid, how much did they come to and if it was gold coins he paid with, where and when did he convert them into cash.

Finally, why would he have left any in the hiding place, which he is supposed to have discovered and how come his servant Marie, who was supposed to be in the know, did not go to get more gold after the death of the Abbe, so as not to live in discomfort until the Corbu family arrived.

There was no treasure at Rennes-le-Chateau and the Abbot Sauniere neither had to look for it or find it.

2 / - Mythology of the Treasure of Rennes.
True story of the Abbot Sauniere vicar of Rennes-le-Chateau.
... Rene Descadeillas - Edition JM Savary ... Carcassonne.
A / Assertions of the author.
Rennes-le-Chateau has had twenty years of publications of stories about a "Treasure".
- It is part of a Classical Mythology about the "Treasure"
(Treasure of Blanche Castille, of the Cathars, of the Temple, of Dagobert).
- Rennes-le-Chateau is a legend.
B / in conclusion, p.129.
- The legend of the Treasure of Rennes comes about because one day a priest came who did not have the right spirit of his profession.
- There have been lots of "searchers" ... hordes of reporters, people fond of hidden symbols, wise men, alchemists ... soliciting shams and multiple depravities at the church and cemetery ... people have gone on about it and made up absurd stories.
All that and why ... for nothing at all.

The above letter and Notes are published with due deference to the Bishop of Carcassonne, who has been reported as saying, - *'The Christian community of our pastoral areas have had more than enough of being the object of curiosity and tall story telling of the whole World'*.
What is really puzzling is why, if those feelings, as expressed by my Lord Bishop and presumably acquiesced by the Church of Rome are based on the words contained in the findings, as laid out in the Authoritative Notes, why long ago was not something done about the situation. The Church of St. Mary Magdalene could so easily be rededicated to its true place in the Christian community ... a House of God, which surely would be most fitting.
In light of the official Church position as expressed in the Notes, it would perhaps be unethical to indulge in too much adverse criticism of those findings and conclusions. However, the moment should not be allowed to pass without a brief comment or two.
The Abbe Bruno de Monts states: -
"There was no treasure at Rennes-le-Chateau and the Abbot Sauniere neither had to look for it nor find it".

Without the text of Bruno de Monts work an assessment as to why he reached that conclusion cannot be made.

He asks 'Where and when'. Because he did not know does not mean there was no treasure. He queries large bills being paid ... so did the Bishop of the day, but paid they were and Sauniere's Bishop wanted to know where the money came from. He asks, 'Why would he leave any in the hiding place'. The author feels that question has been properly answered.

The conclusion of Rene Descadeillas is that the story of the treasure is a legend that has been passed down for generations, and unlikely to be true.

We know there have been lots of searchers, it is an intriguing tale and as those who have taken an active interest in the story know that Sauniere obtained great wealth from somewhere. If it is true Rome or the Holy Roman Emperors paid the priest large sums of money, they must have had very good reasons for doing so; there are probably records to this effect.

During the course of this work it will be suggested that there is more than one treasure. That is to say, all the evidence points to the existence of a second treasure, which I have named as the *Treasure of Arques*. Descadeillas mentions that Cathar as well as the Dagobert treasure is part of the mythology. The Cardinals and Poussin in their day were under no mythical illusions; they had no doubts over the existence of those treasures and Sauniere has confirmed Dagobert's gold existed. More than that, Sir William St. Clair of Rosslyn 'swore by almighty God' there was a great treasure; he built a Chapel dedicated to both. Evidence at Rosslyn confirms the church at Rennes les Bains as the location. Marie Denarnaud witnessed the gold for herself and someone in recent times at Rennes les Bains might also bear testimony to the treasure.

A letter to my Lord Bishop of Carcassonne is ready to post. It will state that Dagobert's gold or *The Treasure of Rennes-le-Chateau* is in the Church of St. Nazaire Et Celse in Rennes les Bains. ... According to the evidence.

CHAPTER 9
BEYOND THE GRAVE

After leaving the Church of St. Mary Magdalene and passing through the archway into the Presbytery courtyard, one pays a few francs to gain entry to the Presbytery, where Sauniere lived and where we found a small Museum. If one was hoping for greater enlightenment from what is on display then there was disappointment. On display were the inverted 'Visigoth' pillar and the imitation Marie de Negri d'Ables Dame D'Hautpoul De Blanchefort head stone that is associated with the Codes and Ciphers; but not much else of real interest.

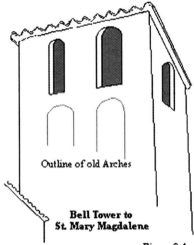

Outline of old Arches

Bell Tower to
St. Mary Magdalene

Figure 9-1

From the Museum I made for the cemetery at the rear of the church to visit the grave of Berenger Sauniere. As was his wish, he is buried in the northwest corner, under the wall that is the boundary with the garden of the Villa Bethanie. The site of his grave and the brief inscription on the headstone holds his last earthly pointer to his treasure; to his right lies Marie Denarnaud remains. His grave had latterly been refurbished; the original grave slab became broken by the ravages of time and over enthusiastic attention by *'multiple depravities at the church and cemetery'*. Fresh roses were there when I last visited, indicating that someone regularly tended the burial place. The choice of his resting-place was quite specific and in keeping with other details. When one stands at the head of his grave and looks southeastwards past the northeast corner of the bell-tower of the church, the line of sight would be on a bearing of 103 degrees, the same as the bearing from Rennes-le-Chateau to St. Nazaire Et Celse.

It was evident in 1996 when I was standing in the lower part of the cemetery and looking back up at the church the Bell Tower in particular showed signs of having been altered at some stage. Below the present bell arches there were indications of earlier lower openings. These are shown in the sketch based on a photograph at that time. The following year work was in progress on the tower and the outlines of the old arches were no longer visible.

Berenger Sauniere died at the age of sixty-five years, under circumstances that are not altogether clear. Had the course of events been otherwise he might have lived another ten years to enjoy his wealth. ... It was not to be. Before the arrival of the new Bishop of Carcassonne,

Monseigneur de Beausejour, Sauniere had enjoyed a comfortable lifestyle more or less free to carry out his plans at St Mary Magdalene. Bishop Billard had been a tolerant man, but de Beausejour was determined to bring his errant priest to heel and particularly after 1908 made life for Sauniere as unpleasant as possible.

Around 1911 Sauniere was relieved of his parish title at St Mary Magdalene and forbidden to administer the Sacraments. Under considerable stress he sought sanctuary and a cure for the deterioration in his mental and physical condition at Lourdes. Sauniere returned to Rennes-le-Chateau refreshed and keen to undertake new projects with plans for the village which included piped water to every home ... plans that were not to be realised.

It is rumoured that shortly before Sauniere suffered a heart attack on 20th January 1917 he had received sinister visitors. Sauniere was not expected to last the night and his friend the priest of Esperaza was sent for to hear his last confession. In the event he lingered on for a few days more but did not recover and died on 22nd January. Whatever it was that Sauniere confessed to on his deathbed it shocked his friend who became too ill to continue with his duties for several months.

Sauniere had understood Poussin's lay out of clues to the treasure. He had correctly interpreted the symbol on Parchment One in relation to the painting, as will be evident in examination of his Stations of the Cross, Statues and the Altar in St Mary Magdalene. He was determined to set out his clues to the treasure and spent a deal of time and a small fortune to achieve his aims. The exterior as well as the interior of the church is adorned with his handiwork and now we see it in the site of his grave and the simple inscription on his headstone. Although the priest's grave slab has been renewed the priest's headstone is original and should not go unnoticed. In comparison, Nicolas Poussin's memorial is both elaborate and informative, whilst Sauniere's takes the form of a plain cross with what appears to be an uninformative epitaph.

The Latin inscription on the headstone is intended to read, *INRI*, an abbreviation for 'Jesus Nazarenus Rex Indaeorum', which Pontius Pilate ordered to be written and placed on the cross over the head of Jesus, during the crucifixion. It means, 'Jesus of Nazareth King of the Jews'; words to which the Jews objected. Pilate retorted, "What I have written, I have written". Maybe the symbol on Sauniere's headstone expresses a similar definitive statement, yet one, which contains a message not at first recognised.

In fact, the second letter, the 'N' in Sauniere's epitaph is reversed as 'И' (ИИRI), with the first downward stroke of the letter resembling a 'J'; something which is clearly designed to attract attention.

Stanley James notes that in the garden to St Mary Magdalene is a Calvaire or 'Calvary' which shows Jesus on the cross and inscribed above his head are the letters 'INRI'. He goes on to split the letters so that the fist and last letters 'I' become the two distant hills the Berque Grande and the Berque Petite. The letters 'N' and 'R' are also split to reveal that between them (alphabetically) are found the 'O' and the 'P', which he uses to demonstrate as meaning *pure gold* and *pure silver*. Exactly what happens to the letter 'Q' is not mentioned. The implication of this exercise is to point us to the treasure being somewhere in the hills.

The title *Jesus Nazarenus* is not far removed from *St. Nazaire* and although Sauniere is not claiming the title for himself, he is using it as a pointer from beyond the grave. He might not have spotted all the coded messages in the Parchment texts, but he did understand the lines through the hills and the parchment symbols, and it is one of these lines, the *lower tail* of the Parchment One symbol, which he has reused, as Poussin has done for a directional pointer.

When Sauniere built the Calvary he may not have had in mind his final clue, but in doing so he had nothing to lose by the inscription on his own *Calvaire*. In essence it is the most simple of headstones with an intriguing and enigmatic epitaph. We see ИИRI but may read INRI and begin to decipher the message. When each 'I' is seen, not as Stanley James's hills, but as inverted commas we have … (')NR('). The 'N' and the 'R' are not split, but taken to mean ... 'N*azaire* R*ennes*'.

Sauniere's last unspoken words tell us … *The Treasure of Rennes-le-Chateau is in the Church of St Nazaire Et Celse at Rennes les Bains.*

The priest was not alone in leaving enigmatic inscriptions on headstones. When the Abbe Boudet left the Presbytery at Rennes les Bains in April 1914 he retired to his old family home at Axat. His illness took its toll on fading health and he died less than a year later. He was buried with his brother at Axat. It is said the tomb has an unusual headstone, which bears the inscription 'IXOIS' that probably refers to Jesus - St Nazaire ET Celse.

In the cemetery to the church at Rennes les Bains, which was severely damage in the inundation of 1992, is a Boudet grave containing the remains of the Abbe's Mother and Sister. The odd thing about the tomb is its orientation, it appears to be pointing at a particular part of the church; its bearing reminiscent of the of 103 degrees line through the hills. The curious inscription on Boudet's tomb and the orientation of the other may add weight to the belief that the priest of Rennes les Bains knew of Dagobert's gold.

CHAPTER 10
DAGOBERT'S GOLD

Dagobert 11, who was effectively the last king of the Merovingian lineage, was born in 652 AD the son of Sigebert 111. His ancestry may be traced back beyond his father, through Dagobert 1 to Alaric the Visigoth who sacked Rome in 410 AD. When he was only two or three years of age Dagobert was sent off to a monastery in Ireland where he stayed for twenty years. His father had died in 656 but due to political wrangling he was not recalled from Ireland to become King until 674 AD. On his return to France he lived at Reddae where his second marriage was to a Visigoth Princess. As a result of his religious upbringing he was sometimes called Saint Dagobert.

During his brief reign as King, Dagobert 11 was famed for his love of justice even though he was greedy and despite his religious upbringing he lacked moral restraint and self-discipline. Even so, he was prosperous and encouraged the arts and learning.

It was whilst hunting in the Forest of Woevres in Lorraine northern France, on the day of the winter solstice in December AD 679 that he met an untimely death. His assailants murdered him whilst he slept by plunging a spear through his eyes. At his death he was only 29 years of age and his reign had lasted just four years after his coming to the throne. The motive for his murder is unclear but probably brought about as a result of political or religious rivalry. Whatever the cause his death it led to the nominal unity of all the Frankish lands under Theodoric111.

The Merovingian King Dagobert 1 founded the Abbey of Saint Denis in 626 on the site regarded as the burial place of Saint Denis, the patron Saint of France. Traditionally it was the place where the Kings of France were interred and it might have been expected that Dagobert 11's remains would also be buried in the Abbey; it was not to be. After his death Dagobert's enemies made every attempt to blot out his name, to write him out of history and to deny his very existence. When he was killed his head was severed and never recovered. His headless skeletal remains were then taken back to Reddae for burial and some time later placed with his treasure at Rennes les Bains. … '*He is there dead*'. There seems no reason to believe that at the time his remains were at Reddae they were interred in the place where Sauniere later discovered a few items of jewellery under the slab referred to as the *Knights Tombstone.*

An unresolved mystery surrounds the *Knights Tombstone,* which is said by some to depict Dagobert attempting to escape his assassins whilst carrying his infant son Sigibert to safety. A loyal companion accompanies him. The picture on the stone also shows a tree and dogs over the arches to complete the hunting scene. The arches resemble those that may be seen in the Chateau Hautpoul at Rennes-le-Chateau where Dagobert once lived.

Sketch of Knight's Tombstone

Figure 10-1

However, whilst it may be a relief picture of Dagobert the stone does not necessarily date from the seventh century. The church and the Chateau was the domain of the Knights Templar around 1185 and it is clear the stone is part of a message associated with whatever was on the parchment found in the newel post. As there is no certainty of when Dagobert's remains were interred with his treasure, and as the stone it did not conceal a grave, only a few items beneath of little value, it is all rather speculative. What appears to be the case is that after Sauniere had made the discovery he set about his nighttimes exploratory digs in the cemetery. Sauniere had misunderstood the information on the piece of parchment together with the picture on the Tombstone and was digging in the wrong place. The Templar knew that Dagobert's headless remains were with his treasure and it was they who under duress told their torturers where Dagobert's treasure was located. As a consequence Poussin was able to relate the information in the Parchments. The Tombstone has all the hallmarks of being Templar, is therefore twelfth century and appears to be directing us to other than Dagobert's gold. However the information uncovered by Sauniere in his church, even if it was still recalled by the Templar was not at the time of the 1307 plot divulged to their inquisitors.

Centuries after the death of Dagobert, around 1646, a date that may be more than coincidental with that inscribed on the porch of Mary Magdalene, a certain Adrien de Valois sought to restore Dagobert's name to its rightful place in history. It was about this time when Nicolas Poussin was thought to have visited the area and set up the Tomb of Arques, the Standing Stone and prepared his sketches for various paintings. It was also about the time the painter was designing and installing the new Altar in St Mary Magdalene; Poussin was not aware of the Knights Tombstone or the newel parchment and reference to it does not appear in the Altar Parchments. Having said that there is always the possibility that the excess letters on Parchment Two do contain a coded message.

As early as the 5th century the Visigoths, often at other friendly countries expense, were taking every opportunity to extend their territory. They established kingdoms in Gaul and Spain and in 475 the Visigoth Euric declared himself an independent king, with his capital at Toulouse. It was under him that the Gallic kingdom reached its widest extent, stretching from the Loire to the Pyrenees and to the lower reaches of the Rhône River, including the greater portion of Spain. The defeat at the battle of Vouillé by the Franks meant that the Visigoths lost all their possessions in Gaul apart from Septimania, a strip of land stretching along the coast from the Pyrenees to the Rhône, with Narbonne as its capital, which the Franks were never able to take from them. The Visigoths continued to rule parts of Septimania and Spain, until finally driven out by the Muslims in 711 AD.

Figure 10-2

After the fall and sacking of Rome in 410 AD the Visigoths divided their treasures, which had amassed over the years and included spoils taken from Jerusalem by the Romans under Titus in 70AD. A small part of that treasure was later discovered in the Spanish province of Toledo. The greater part remained and was later to become known as Dagobert's gold. The hoard consisted of some of the earliest Visigoth treasure, a part of the Jerusalem Temple treasure and a considerable amount of coinage and other valuables plundered from the citizens of Rome. The largest item looted by the Romans in Jerusalem was the Menorah, which required four or five men to carry it. This item according to Poussin, Sauniere and Stanley James is with the Treasure of Rennes-le-Chateau and therefore at St Nazaire ET Celse, to this day. However, certain Knights, such as Hugh de Payen and André de Montbard, presumably through family connections, were aware of the content of Dagobert's hoard and realised that the Romans who had plundered Jerusalem had discovered and removed little of the Temple treasure. The whereabouts of a huge amount of gold and silver as well as the most important Temple artefacts, including the Ark of the Covenant (the Holy Grail) was still a mystery and the Knights, under false pretences went to Jerusalem to search for it.

Stanley James, reading Sauniere, suggests there is the possibility of later Templar treasure being added to Dagobert's gold; this appears to be supported by reference to Rennes les Bains in Rosslyn Chapel by the Knight Templar Sir William St Clair.

In 1118, the two knights, along with seven companions, all with family connections, presented themselves to King Baldwin Il the Patriarchs of Jerusalem. They announced that it was their intention to found an order of warrior monks who would keep the roads and highways safe for the protection of pilgrims to the Holy Land. The order took vows of personal poverty and chastity and to hold all their property in common. The king gave them quarters in the stables of what was believed to be part of the Temple of Solomon complex and granted the new order of knights the right to wear the double barred Cross of Lorraine as their insignia.

The large sum of monies paid to Sauniere by Rome was for an item of considerable importance. If it was part of the original hoard or if something added to the treasure by the Templar, the Church seemed unaware of its existence. They would not have been interested in possessing the *menorah* or silver trumpets that Stanley James implies are with the hoard. Nor would they have wanted gold or precious stones. A romantic notion may suggest it was the *cup of the last supper*, the Holy Grail that was on offer and if so would not have been difficult for Sauniere to remove with or without the Abbe Boudet consent.

Over the course of a thousand years from Dagobert to Boudet the location of the treasure was known to a few in successive generations and undoubtedly there were those who succumbed to the temptation and from time to time had raided the sanctuary. It fell to the Abbes' Boudet and Sauniere to help them to a considerable amount of the treasure. Between them, when it can be imagined that for thirty or more years they had free access to a great deal of gold in the form of coins, rings, ornaments and precious stones, particularly Boudet, they had sold off much of the *loose change*. Even so, much may still remain, including valuable items such as the Menorah and perhaps the item for which Rome paid so much money.

SAUNIERE'S SECRETS

CHAPTER 11
ASMODEUS

It was a beautiful day in June 1897 when the Bishop of the clergy of the Upper Aude Valley arrived at the Church of St. Mary Magdalene at Rennes-le-Chateau. Dignitaries from the village together with their beaming priest Berenger Sauniere were there to greet him. After a few pleasantries were exchanged the Bishop was invited to lead his flock into the Church for the inauguration ceremony.

Pausing for a moment before entering the church his eminence, Monseigneur Billard the Bishop of Carcassonne, might have taken note of the inscription above the porch, 'My House shall be called the house of prayer'. The Bishop may even have been pleased to see his heraldic device alongside that of the Pope, but to read above the door, 'This place is terrible' must have given him cause for concern. Imagine the Bishop's sense of shock when having passed through the Porch he is confronted by the *Devil;* it could hardly have put His Eminence in the best frame of mind and he never again returned to the church at Rennes-le-Chateau.

When last I visited the church Asmodeus the Devil statue that supports the Holy Water Stoup or Le Benitier was in a poor state of repair. It had stood there for eighty years and the ravages of time and rough handing had left their marks.

It has been suggested the statue represents the demon that once guarded Solomon's treasure at Jerusalem. The figure is half squatting in a pose that looks twisted and uncomfortable, with its' right hand index finger and thumb appearing to form the shape of the letter 'O'. Above the Devil's head is a Water Stoup; over which are two Salamanders and above them is the now obliterated monogram that originally bore the letters 'BS'. The plinth over the monogram is inscribed with the (translated) words, *'By this sign ye shall conquer him'*, and atop the statue are four Angels, who between them are making the sign of the cross.

The top Angels is looking into the distance towards Station One of the Cross; the Angel on ones left has a pose which resembles that of the statue of Mary Magdalene, with the right hand angel gazing towards the statue of John the Baptist, above les Fonts Baptismaux. The last angel is staring at the Altar, with her left hand pointing down to the inscription on the plinth.

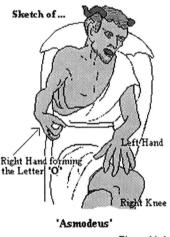

'Asmodeus'

Figure 11-1

The monogram and the Salamanders are linked. The initials could mean Berenger Sauniere, but probably they indicate the two rivers, the B*lanque* and the S*als*, which converge at the pool known as the Holy Water Stoup, by the bridge just south of Rennes les Bains.

Stanley James suggests that the word *Salamanders* may be written in anagram form as, *Sals a mandre*, where the 'a' is silent, leaving us with *Sals and mandre*, which he says means, *'The River Sals going south east to the Tour de la Mandre'*. James is convinced the treasure is in a cave somewhere in the vicinity of the hills, la Berco Grando and la Berco Petito. He believes the pictures in Sauniere's Stations of the Cross provide clues to a trail that commences at Rennes les Bains and leads him into the hills. James continues the theme as he analyses Asmodeus. The Fanthorpe's mention little of Asmodeus except to say he is regarded as the guardian of

Solomon's treasure and sometimes referred to as Rex Mundi. It was Henry Lincoln who offered the more interesting approach and prompted me to visit the location of *The Devil's Armchair*

The statue Asmodeus is depicted sitting in what is taken to be *Le Fauteuil du Diable* or 'The Devil's Armchair'. It is a large carved stone boulder near the *Spring of the Circle,* on the hillside just south of Rennes les Bains; two and three quarter miles from Rennes-le-Chateau, but less than half a mile from St. Nazaire Et Celse.

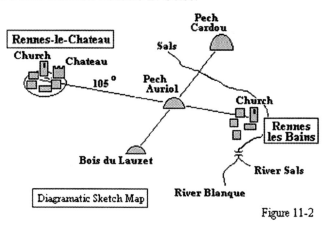

Figure 11-2

The Devil's right hand is thought by some to have once held a trident, but this seems impractical and unlikely given the shape of the hand. If the gesture is mimicked it is clear one would be indicating the formation of the letter 'O', which could be taken as the first letter of the French word for gold, namely OR. The Devil's left hand is on his bare right knee; the French word for kneecap is, *rotule.* The Devil's right leg covers the left knee, it is right over left and the priest is inviting us to read from right to left, with the over large hand resting on the right knee emphasising the point. If we were to reverse the word *rotule*, we would then read '*elut*OR', with the last two letters completing the word for gold. When the letter 't' is silent we are left with the French word 'elu', meaning 'elected' or 'chosen', which is not far removed from Poussin's language in the Parchments when he refers to, '*The corn of Redis* (is) *only for the priesthood*' (Lincoln).

We are intended to see Asmodeus in the Devil's Armchair in which he is perched rather awkwardly on the front left-hand edge of the seat, on a diagonal that appears to be facing the valley, which runs north and south. The statue is turned with a downward facing gaze at the town below. If the clues presented in *Le Benitier* are being read correctly, they form a comprehensive and pointed direction sign ... *By this sign ...* to the church at Rennes les Bains.

Geoffrey Morgan

Fleury Tableau

Les Berger's d'Arcadie (The Arcadian Shephers)

Plate 5

Cardou

Church Tower

The Hill Auriol

Bois du Lauzet

Plate 6

CHAPTER 12
THE FLEURY TABLEAU

High on the West wall, above the Confessional in the Church of St Mary Magdalene is the Fleury Tableau or, Le Grand Haut Relief. It is an imposing work of art and dominates the Nave. The Tableau symbolizes a simple message which is ... 'Come unto me'. Along the bottom edge of the huge picture are the words ... 'Venez a Moi Vous tous qui souffrey et qui accables et je vous Soulagerai'; which roughly translates as, *'All come to the design under the frieze to seek the bag of earth* (gold) *I have seen in an enlarged width low down'*. Stanley James suggests it might be translated as, *'Come unto me all who labour and are overwhelmed and I will give you* (a life of) *ease'*. It is an open invitation for anyone to come and look and understand what Sauniere has to tell.

VOUS TOUS QUI SOUFFREZ ET QUI ETES ACCABLES
VENEZ A MOI   ET JE VOUS SOULAGERAI

The Fleury Tableau
On the west wall of the Nave above the Confessional

Figure 12-1

The central section of the tableau is in bas-relief with the backdrop starting from the springing of the arch. It has the underlying shape of a mound or small hill, quite steep and could be likened to the outcrop on which Rennes-le-Chateau sits. Atop of the hill stands the figure of Christ with arms outstretched in a gesture that is saying, 'Come unto me', whilst below Him on the hill is a representative faction of a community. At the foot of the hill is a bag that has split open to reveal a coin.

Roses that cascade beneath the feet of Christ are reminiscent of the roses in the apron of the statue of St. Germaine. To the left of the relief, above the words, '*Venez a Moi* ' one gets the impression of water amongst the rocks. On the other side above the word, '*Soulagerai*', is a skull. Directly above the skull is a figure, probably walking with the aid of a stick, with a village in the background. Sauniere may be telling us to go to the distant village by the water where there is an old and infirm person. The skull in the picture nestles against the capital of a fallen colonnade, parts of which are arranged to look like crossbones.

As a starting point and the opening that sets the scene to Sauniere's clues, the importance of the Tableau is easily overlooked. Stanley James in his book carefully analyses every detail. His reading is that the Tableau points towards the hills Berque Grando and Berque Petito and he uses the picture in Station '1' of the Cross to describe events at Rennes les Bains, with the trail continuing through the pictures to the hills. However Henry Lincoln differs and places Station 'V1' at Rennes-le-Chateau. In the event both assumptions are incorrect, as examination of the remaining Stations will demonstrate.

Christ is on a hill and there are two women kneeling at His feet. The older woman on his left has her head in her hands; she is hiding her eyes. The younger woman on His right is holding on to Christ's garment and looking intently down the hill ... she is Mary Magdalene. Behind the older woman, Mary Mother of Jesus, is a priest who holds out his hands as if offering something.

As one gazes up at the Tableau he or she is immediately in front of the Confessional - 'Come unto me' ... not to confess, but to hear a tale, a priest's *confession*. The roles are to be reversed; the 'sinner' or treasure seeker is not there to confess, but to hear a story. Through his pictures and statues he will lead us to Dagobert's gold ... the *Treasure of Rennes-le-Chateau*.

The casual visitor is at first uncertain of what to expect when entering St. Mary Magdalene. There are no signs, no obvious pointers as to where to commence ones quest. The official guide relates only the well-rehearsed and old familiar story and there is much in Sauniere's work that is designed to dazzle and confuse the treasure seeker. Others for all their expertise fair little better in attempts to unravel the mystery in the many works, which have been written on the subject.

It is time for a fresh approach, to listen to what the priest is actually saying to us. '*Stand at the Confessional and look around; look down the Nave, stop and think for a moment ... read the pictures*'.

CHAPTER 13
THE STATIONS OF THE CROSS

The Church of St Mary Magdalene has been a place of mystery since 1892. Over the Porch it is written, 'Terribilis Est'...*This place is terrible.* To the casual visitor, congregation and Clergy who hold such a place in reverence the legacy of Sauniere is indeed *terrible*. The Church that after all is a House of God is full of paraphernalia in the guise of traditional objects of worship; but *ye have made it a den of thieves.*

Clues to the treasure are seen to be everywhere, at the entrance, on the Altar and in the statues and Stations of the Cross. With such an abundance of clues left to us by the priest it should have been child's play to crack the code. Poussin used his paintings and simple Parchment sketches, Sauniere also talks to us in pictures, which as set out in this work are surprisingly easy to follow.

Being confident of where the treasure can be located was a considerable advantage in determining what Sauniere has set out in his pictures and earlier assumptions that it would not be possible to resolve the pictures in the Stations proved unfounded. My interpretation of the pictures may appear matter-of-fact and over simplified, even complacent, but it seems to work and like Sauniere I arrived at my conclusions by following Poussin. It may be stating the obvious but without first understanding Poussin and locating the treasure the priest could not have set out his clues in the way he has.

In Fig 13.10 all the Stations of the Cross are set out to show the sequence that Sauniere adopted in planning his route through the hills to the site of the treasure. Poussin's symbol on Parchment One, in relation to his painting Les Berger's d'Arcadie, was the key to unraveling *Sauniere's Code*. Both Henry Lincoln and Stanley James demonstrated their skills at reading Sauniere's pictures by employing language. At first I was convinced that on that basis I could not resolve the pictures and no attempt was made to examine them.

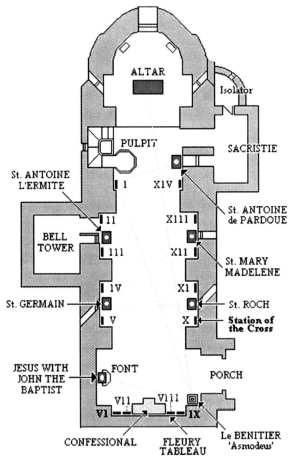

PLAN of the CHURCH of St. MARY MAGDALENE
at RENNES - LE - CHATEAU

Figure 13-1

However, the drawing of Fig 13.1 – the plan of St Mary Magdalene – enabled me to see the pairing of the Stations within the Church and the possibility of a sequence of steps. This proved not to be straightforward, but it did lead to my reading of the pictures as Sauniere intended. I would not have been the first person to see familiar landmarks in Sauniere's pictures. The hill Cardou dominates the area around Rennes-le-Chateau and can be easily recognised in Station X1. Henry Lincoln in describing Station V1 must have prompted others to attempt reading the pictures and anyone knowing the topography of the area and St Nazaire Et Celse could begin to understand Sauniere's clues. Stanley James' description of Station X1 is colourful with use of anagrams manipulating Sauniere's picture in an endeavour to point to the hills Berque Grande and Berque Petite, where he is convinced the treasures lies. He uses the ladder in the picture as a scale of height and distance and the pole with the silver discs he sees as medallions associated with Asmodeus and the Bigou Cipher.

The sketch layout of the church shows the location of the icons and Stations that are found arranged along the north, south and west walls of the Nave. Station '1' is at the eastern end immediately before the Pulpit and the Chancel, with Station 'X1V' set opposite on the south wall. As one returns down the Nave towards the back of the church, on the right the picture numbers increase from '1' to 'V', and on the left, decrease from 'X1V' to 'X.' - Stations 'V1', 'V11', 'V111' and '1X' are on the rear or west wall; two either side of the Confessional. Sauniere planned a traditional layout of the Stations and although on that basis one might logically expect clues to the whereabouts of the treasure to commence with Station '1' and reach its conclusion with Station 'X1V' the priest carefully avoided the *obvious.*

Henry Lincoln has interpreted Station 'V1' as, *'at the bottom of the enclosure one should then make a half turn towards Cardou'*; the observer is then looking at the crest. However, Lincoln took the enclosure to mean the Cemetery at St. Mary Magdalene, not the enclosure or triangle that is made by the heads of the three shepherds ... namely, Rennes-le-Chateau, Bois du Lauzet and Auriol. Half a turn at Bois du Lauzet does find one facing the crest of Cardou.

Assuming there is a pattern for us to follow in Sauniere's placing of the Stations, we must first look for a starting point. The Fleury Tableau appeared to be directing us towards the Confessional, either side of which under the West wall are the unpaired Stations. As we stand in front of the Confessional with our backs to the wall looking down the Nave, on ones left, along the wall, are Stations 'V11' and 'V1'. On the other side of the Confessional are the Stations 'V111' and '1X'. Traditionally the Stations of the Cross show progression from Pilate to Golgotha and the Sepulchre, but Sauniere gives us pictures that are full of double meaning. Jesus is symbolised by Sauniere, sometimes as the Christ and at other times as the *treasure seeker.* In the picture to Station '1' Jesus is before Pilate. In the last picture, Station 'X1V' he shows the body of Jesus being carried towards a cave in a large rock to which we appear directed.

The scene in Station 'V11' is of the second fall of Jesus; Station 'V1' depicts the woman Veronica wiping His face. In Station 'V111' Jesus speaks to the distressed women and in Station '1X', according to Scripture, Jesus has fallen for the third time. We could expect no help from Sauniere and are left to find the start of the treasure trail using our own initiative. The thought that being at the Confessional was where we might commence our journey was based on a hunch. It was possible that here we would find a clue to help us on our way. As Station 'V11' and Station 'V111' are the closest pictures to the Confessional one of them may prove to be the starting point.

STATION V111   Figure 13-2

At the outset of a journey friends and relatives may gather to say farewell to the person about to depart; there were such people around Jesus when He set off for Calvary. This in effect appears to be what Sauniere is portraying in Station 'V111'. Jesus had been before Pilate who found no fault in him, but to appease the Jews the Roman governor took a bowl of water and washed his hands of the whole affair; the act depicted by Sauniere in Station '1'.

In Station 'V111', which is considered to be our first step, Jesus is standing with the cross, the western arm of which is touching the head of

Mary Magdalene; He is bidding her farewell. We the treasure-seeker must leave Rennes-le-Chateau and go away in the direction in which the Soldier is looking. He is the soldier behind the eastern arm of the crosspiece with the southern upright facing southeast - pointing the way; the direction is clear. Half way between east and south puts us on a bearing for Bois du Lauzet.

STATION VII   Figure 13-3

Station 'VII' is our second step. … In this picture Jesus is on His knees and looking intently down at a mound. It is the place in Scripture of His second fall. The mound is Rennes-le-Chateau and the west end of the crosspiece rests on that hill; the east arm of the cross points to a tower. The figure on the right is trying to pull Jesus up, whilst another is attempting to lift the wooden cross and move it off the hill, away from the west and Rennes-le-Chateau. The first person on the left is holding his arm aloft, indicating an upward direction. Above his head is the Roman Standard with three discs. The spear is alongside the lower disc, but pointing to the middle disc that is one of the three hills. The higher disc is Cardou; the middle disc represents Auriol and the lower one is the hill on which Jesus' foot is resting. All the characters in the picture are looking down at the mound. Sauniere's sketch is unmistakable in its intent. Jesus is being urged by all around him to *get up*, to *move on*. We must also go, for the treasure is not at Reddae.

STATION 'IX' Figure 13-4

In the Scriptures, Station'1X' describes the third fall of Jesus, which is our third step. Here Sauniere has used it to show Jesus immediately after the fall in Station 'V11'. He is still on the ground, on the slope of Rennes-le-Chateau. His legs are on the smaller hill and He is no longer looking at the mound; His back is turned to it and a soldier is pulling Him to His feet. He must stand up and when He does He will be on Bois du Lauzet. A second soldier is lifting the cross off the hill, the western arm is hidden from view and we see the eastern arm is touching the Centurion (Titus) on the horse. The treasure-seeker is to leave St Mary Magdalene and go to the small hill it is the second Shepherd in Poussin's painting.

[Titus was born AD 40, sacked and destroyed Jerusalem in AD 70 and became Roman Emperor from AD 79 to 81].

Jesus kneels on
a slight mound.
- Bois du Lauzet

STATION 'VI'   Figure 13-5

Station 'VI' is our step number four. Sauniere's clues although appearing haphazard are following a pattern; in this picture Jesus is recovering from his fall. He is kneeling on a slight mound, which is the *bottom of the enclosure*, the hill Bois du Lauzet. The foot of the cross is out of the picture, going south is no longer an option. Jesus is in a very weak physical state and does not immediately stand upon His feet after collapsing on the ground.

Veronica of the cloth is wiping Jesus' forehead as He kneels. His head is in line with Veronica's and that of the soldier holding the shield, with his back to us. Veronica represents the middle hill Auriol; Jesus is Bois du Lauzet and the high soldier is Cardou. The other soldier with his hand on Veronica's shoulder draws attention to her importance. Simon, on the other side of the cross is also looking at Veronica; Sauniere is pointing us to the next step.

Simon
of Cyrène

STATION 'V'   Figure 13-6

In Station 'V', which is our step five, Jesus is once more on the move. The picture to hand of Station 'V' shows a certain amount of damage and consequently some detail is lost. Jesus is up and walking away from Bois du Lauzet, whilst holding the upwardly inclined cross below the cross-member, with Simon Cyrene ahead of Him supporting the weight.

All the characters in the picture are facing the same direction. Simon's left hand is at the top of the cross, telling us the way is towards the high point. There are three heads in a line; the soldier at the rear with his left arm lowered is Bois du Lauzet. Jesus in the middle is now Auriol and Simon is Cardou. The western arm of the wooden cross is out of the picture, on to the frame, as if to indicate that direction is no longer to be considered.

STATION 'IV'   Figure 13-7

Station 'IV' is our sixth step. In this picture Jesus is carrying the cross and holding the hand of His mother Mary; Mary Magdalene is kneeling and Simon Cyrene is in front of Jesus between the north and west arms of the cross, he is reaching around the woodwork to pull Jesus away from the women. We are beyond the point of no return. In the background is a vertical pole from which hangs a white sheet set at an angled of 45 degrees. The three silver discs are in a vertical line with the top disc at the highest point of the sheet and the lower one partially hidden. This indicates we have moved away from the lower hill and there is no looking back. Simon is tugging at His shirt, pulling Jesus towards Auriol that is Golgotha. Sauniere's footstep's plot our progress through the Stations of the Cross and leads us away from his church of St. Mary Magdalene on a trail that although not exactly following the line set out by the Parchment One symbol, uses the general directions to take us to the treasure.

The priest had set himself a difficult task and there were probably moments after he had completed his work when he must have felt he had given the game away too easily. He need not have concerned himself for apart from the early days when the Abbe Gelis and possibly the Abbe Rescanieres came close to finding the treasure a whole century has passed and still his secret appears to be safe. Having said that there are suspicions that the Church Authorities and perhaps those who conspired to formulate the so-called Bigou Codes and Ciphers know where the treasure is located.

Sauniere's pictures in his Stations of the Cross, which are so prominent in the church of Mary Magdalene, appear to be ignored by most commentators and until now, no one other than Henry Lincoln and Stanley James has attempted to read them.

STATION 'X'   Figure 13-8

The picture in Station 'X' is step number seven and we find ourselves at Golgotha or Auriol, the *Place of a Skull*, where our Lord was being disrobed and crucified. One soldier is behind Him holding His outer garment to project an outline resembling Cardou. The kneeling soldier has his left foot on an upturned shield. It is not held high as in Station 'VI'. We are no longer at the lower hill. Jesus' garment is at midpoint about His waist and His left arm is extended low with the palm towards us ... He is directing us to observe the kneeling soldier whose pose, although handed, is that of the second shepherd in Poussin's painting. Five soldiers are around Him casting lots for His raiment. Two dice are on the ground showing on the one face the '3' and on an adjoining face a '4', which of course is not possible on a dice; the figure '5' shows on the second dice.

The wooden cross is almost out of the picture and we ignore it for directional purposes. The figures '3', '4' and '5' are well known in mathematical terms as representing a right-angled triangle, a bearing. ...

The '3' and '4' are east and north. The line from Bois du Lauzet through Auriol to Cardou is on a bearing of 46 degrees and the triangle is not strictly right-angled but close enough for us to understand the message in the dice.

STATION 'XI'   Figure 13-9

The priest had plenty of time to consider how he would present his clues and must have enjoyed himself with many a light hearted moment as he reviewed his handiwork. I am intrigued as to where his workshop might have been. It is evident the pictures, frames, plinths and statues occupied a sizeable storage area before they were finally installed in the redecorated church. Not to mention the Altar and the huge Fleury Tableau; it was a colossal undertaking.

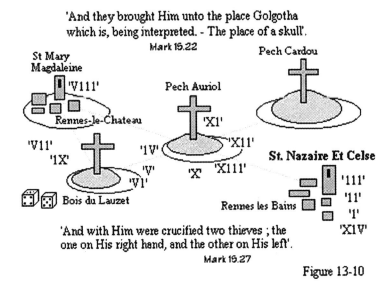

'And they brought Him unto the place Golgotha
which is, being interpreted. - The place of a skull'.
Mark 15.22

'And with Him were crucified two thieves ; the
one on His right hand, and the other on His left'.
Mark 15.27

Figure 13-10

Station 'X1' is our eighth step and we are at Auriol or *Calvary* where the lines intersect on the bearings 103 and 46 degrees. The cross is on the ground with Jesus being laid upon it. The soldier behind the ladder is holding a Standard with the silver discs set against the dark outline shape of Cardou; the discs are the hills, Cardou, Auriol and Bois du Lauzet. The soldier who has his back to us is holding up a ladder by the middle of the top three rungs, once again emphasising the middle hill, with the higher rung in this case being Rennes-le-Chateau and the lower Rennes les Bains. At Calvary Jesus was crucified between the two thieves. The slope of the ladder, although greater than the 103 degrees, brings it in line with the feet of Jesus and the foot of the cross. The soldier's downward pointing foot is also touching the foot of the cross, with the other soldier and Jesus looking at the same spot. The emphasis is on the foot of the cross, the foot of Jesus … it is St Nazaire and it is unmistakable.

In Fig 13.10 all the Stations of the Cross are set out to show the sequence that Sauniere adopted in planning his route through the hills to the site of the treasure. Once he had decided that his arrangement of the clues within the pictures should be based on the Stations and as far as possible the Parchment One symbol he had established a pattern. In fact it was a clever idea and all that was required was to adapt the traditional pictures and utilize what Poussin had provided.

The hill Ariol

STATION 'X11'   Figure 13-11

Step nine is Station 'X11', where we find Jesus on the cross after the act of crucifixion. There are six characters around Him, two soldiers and four women. Here again the photograph to hand is poor quality, although it can be seen one of the women is kneeling at the foot of the cross with both hands grasping something that resembles a bag, immediately under the feet of Jesus; beneath St Nazaire. The first woman on the left is attracting our attention to whatever her kneeling companion is trying to remove. The female on the right is looking up at the Lord, her right hand at her breast, her left hand clutching a closed book. It may be a quirk of light; an illusion, but a skull might be detected in the original picture. It is just above the pointing hand of the first lady, between the second female and the leg of Jesus. All the other characters around the cross are looking at Jesus the *Church*.

The hill Ariol

STATION 'X111'   Figure 13-12

Station 'X111' is our step ten and the setting is still at Auriol. There are no soldiers in this picture only the two women with Joseph of Aramathea and Nicodemus. The body of Jesus is being taken down from the cross; His right arm is held high, but below the crosspiece. We are on our way down from Auriol; His left arm is hanging down at the level of His feet and pointing to the hands of the female who in Station 'X11' was attempting to remove the bag under His feet. The figure on the ladder is holding a white vestment, which is above the crosspiece and suggests the crest of Cardou.

We are now to move on from Auriol and this may be the moment to halt our journey through the Stations of the Cross and concentrate instead on what the Statues have to tell us.

St Nazaire Et Celse from River

St Nazaire Et Celse

Plate 7

Geoffrey Morgan

The Bridge at Rennes les Bains

Site of
Old 'Tomb of Arques'

Plate 8

CHAPTER 14
THE STATUES

Having dealt separately with Le Benitier or Asmodeus we now turn our attention to the remainder of the statues Sauniere has arranged around the walls of the church. The first statue is that of 'Jesus with John the Baptist', which is located between Stations 'VI' and 'V' on the north side of the Nave. The placing of Statues between the Stations leads one to suspect a connection or link with the pictures and this may have been the priest's intention. However, as the location of the treasure was determined without the aid of Sauniere's Stations of the Cross pictures it seemed unlikely the statues would add anything of value and may have been as a cosmetic ploy by Sauniere to create a distraction.

Station 'VI' has taken us to the hill Bois du Lauzet, while Station 'V' finds us at Auriol. The first statue shows Jesus crouched low with His hands folded in prayer. He is looking down over the water, not at the Font but at something that is below Him, to His right. The church at Rennes les Bains looks down on the water, the River Sals.

Jesus with John the Baptist

Figure 14-1

John the Baptist is standing behind Jesus and gives the impression of pouring water from a seashell – the act of baptism. Yet it is more than that. The shell is kaolin - chalk, the chalky outcrop at the crest of Cardou comes to mind. The head of Jesus is the hill Auriol and the hands in prayer are St Nazaire Et Celse.

We do not see John's eyes, which appear to suggest that although he is taking us to the water we should not look to Cardou but concentrate on what Jesus is doing. This is further emphasised by John who is holding a staff with a cross-member on which is draped a ribbon banner bearing the Latin words, 'ECCE AGNUS DEI' ... *Behold the Lamb of God*. The crosspiece on the staff looks as if it is at an angle of 103 degrees and represents the line through the hills from Rennes-le-Chateau. The left hand or western top of

102

the crosspiece and the ribbon is effectively obscuring John's vision, which may be Sauniere's way of telling us we will *see no treasure* at Rennes-le-Chateau. The statue might also be seen as comprising a direction pointer with the staff and the crosspiece and the shell, the head of Jesus and his hands.

Saint Roch

Figure 14-2

We then move down and across the Nave to the statue of St Roch that is placed between Stations 'X' and 'XI' and appears to be facing across the Nave at St. Germaine. In Station 'X' Christ is being disrobed and in 'XI' he is at the point of crucifixion. Both Stations have Cardou on the left of the cross with Rennes les Bains straight-ahead, on a bearing of 103 degrees. St. Roch worked among the poor and was the patron saint of those with plague. Sauniere has the saint showing a bare right leg to reveal the three joints, the hip the knee and the ankle The toe of the boot is touching the sheep's foot; its head is level with the saint's knee, but looking up at a wound in his leg. The priest undoubtedly had his reasons for including this statue, but as far as one can judge it contributes little if anything to the quest for the treasure.

Figure 14-3

Across the Nave of the church we find Saint Germaine, the shepherdess who has sheep at her feet and her apron is full of roses [Sauniere grew roses]. She stands between Stations 'V' and '1V' and is looking affectionately back across the Nave at Mary Magdalene. These Stations are in the hills, the place of the shepherds. One of the sheep is attracted by the roses and at the same time is *pointing* at the lower sheep. St. Germaine is Sauniere's portrait of Marie and his lasting tribute to a friend and companion. The priest's placing of the Statues may suggest the characters are *communicating* with one another, but it is difficult to know if we are meant to see interaction between the characters. We appear to see it with the four Angels above Asmodeus. St. Roch is looking across at St. Germaine, who in turn is looking at Mary Magdalene. Sauniere has contrived pretence at interaction, either for the purposes of projecting clues or simply to distract. Asmodeus makes a major contribution towards the quest for the treasure, but apart from academic interest the remaining statues may have only limited value.

Marie Madeleine

Figure 14-4

The statue of St. Mary Madeleine, holding an upright cross, stands opposite St. Antoine L'Ermite and is placed between Stations 'X11' and 'X111', the only two pictures where the wooden cross is also shown upright, at Auriol, or Golgotha in the hills. Mary Madeleine is looking across the Nave at Station '1' and holding an urn that may signify death, the Tomb, or the very costly *Ointment of Spikenard* – the treasure. At her foot is a skull resting on an open book. Sauniere's one-time friend the Abbe Boudet had written a book. Sauniere and Boudet's falling out effectively barred the priest of Rennes-le-Chateau further access to the treasure. Using a book as a clue may symbolically be interpreted in St. Antoine de Pardoue, as the priest's way of ridiculing the older man ... a bit of give away to those who associated the two, something that was probably spotted by the Abbe Gelis. The book certainly appears in situations that one would consider relates to the location of the treasure and where one expects to see a book, there is a skull. The Urn Mary Magdalene is holding is similar to that shown in the circular window picture beyond the Altar where Mary is anointing the feet of Jesus with the ointment; another indicator that the treasure is below the *feet* of St Nazaire.

Saint Antoine Ermite

Figure 14-5

St. Antoine L'Ermite lived in a cave, in a tunnel, in a rock, dedicating himself to God; the *Treasure of Rennes-le-Chateau* is in a cave in a hillside via a tunnel. The statue represents Sauniere himself and it stands next to St. Germaine. In the cemetery of St Mary Magdalene we find Sauniere and Marie Denarnaud lie side by side. In his one hand the statue holds a book, in the other a staff with a bell. St. Antoine is also looking across the Nave at Mary Magdalene; Sauniere's church. The statue of St. Antoine de Pardoue stands opposite Mary Magdalene. He was a great preacher and said to have converted many sinners. If this is again Sauniere then he stands holding an open book on which is the infant Christ representing St. Nazaire Et Celse at Rennes les Bains.

St. Antoine de Pardoue

Figure 14-6

The crucifix, in the belt of the statue indicates the lines through the hills. Three Angels on an orb hold aloft the statue. Sauniere is on high, defiant; he has the church with its treasure in his hand. Sauniere's elevated position was short-lived. At his end he was not granted absolution for his sins ... he lost everything, his church, his treasure and his life. In his after-life he might be reflecting on what could have been.

The statues of Saint Joseph and Saint Mary play no part in the quest for the treasure, although others may see things differently and may point to something missed by this work.

CHAPTER 15
THE ALTAR

The Altar in the church of Mary Magdalene could be described as imposing or even over-ornate. In normal circumstances a Communion Table in a small village church would be a simple structure reflecting its status. That would not do for Sauniere, he had a statement to make and the Altar was to play its part. It was after all Poussin's Altar, that as far as the story goes, was where it all began for the priest of Rennes-le-Château and although we might not expect history to repeat itself, it is possible that Sauniere's Altar also contains a secret other than we see presented to us.

Figure 15-1

The Church Altar is the centre of focus and Sauniere's Altar is no exception. However it is not the structure or what may be concealed within it that is of immediate interest, but the lower frontispiece with its bas-relief picture. It is a picture of a young woman at prayer kneeling in water besides a cave set low in a large rock with face-like features. At the entrance to the cave is a skull. A sapling tree with a crosspiece at an angle of 103 degrees grows nearby with its roots close to the water; an open book is over the cave entrance. She divides the water just as the Stone or menhir known as 'de la Madeleine' divides the Blanque and the Sals above the bridge at Rennes les Bains. She is Mary Magdalene and she is looking up at the cross-members, the lines through the hills. The fingers of her hands are prominent and reminiscent of Asmodeus' hands.

The Cardinals of Rome had confided in Poussin and commissioned him to set down on canvas and parchments a burdensome secret. The painter in his turn confided in his friend the Abbe Fouquet who told his brother, who then acquainted the King of France. All of these people could only imagine such wealth. Not so with Sauniere, he achieved the seemingly impossible, yet could confide in no one other than the Abbe Boudet. When Sauniere first talked with Boudet the older man would have no doubt been a little boastful of how he had discovered the treasure and just how long he had known of it. There is no way of knowing if others before him had also found Dagobert's gold. Imagine those first moments when Sauniere had been shown the access point to the treasure, had watched the older man light the lantern and lead him down those old rough hewn steps beneath the church to the entrance to the tunnel. He followed Boudet, crouching low for a few metres and then found himself in a fair sized cavern with the glint of gold all around him. The older man shone the light around and let his younger companion stare is amazement at what was before them. Before they left and after Sauniere had filled his pockets with whatever he could carry Boudet pointed out the skeletal form of King Dagobert 11 ... *and he is there dead.*

Years earlier when Boudet had first ventured down those ancient stone steps and cautiously made his way along the tunnel it must a been a daunting experience. The sight that met his eyes was unbelievable; the gold and silver was everywhere. The sight of the huge gold menorah that had once adorned King Herod's Temple and which was now propped against the cavern wall must have caused his hair to stand on end The shock of so much treasure may even have turned the priest's hair grey over night. The elation of his sudden wealth would be short lived and quickly turn to panic at the prospects of what in that moment was his could all too soon could be taken away from him. Little wonders when Sauniere was ultimately denied access to all that wealth he was driven to such passions. The Abbe Boudet kept his composure and did not initially over indulge himself with the temptation that was all around him. Sauniere's arrival on the scene however was not something he would have wished for.

The pictures in the Stations of the Cross at St Mary Magdalene have now been decoded; it was always possible providing one had the right break. The Abbe Gelis found and exploited a weak link in Sauniere's show and it would be surprising if the Church Authorities during the course of the past one hundred years have not also quietly undertaken some serious research into the subject. Reading between the lines of denials in the Church's Authoritative Notes appears to confirm this. The official position is that there is no treasure, but no explanation is offered for the huge sums of money undeniably spent at Rennes-le-Chateau by the errant priest.

If the rumours are founded that an emissary from Austria visited Sauniere during the First World War it could not have happened without the co-operation and knowledge of his Bishop. The Church may be playing a waiting game and that contrary to the official position do privately accept there is a treasure and that it is well documented.

This work makes no secret of where the treasure may be found; it is as set down by Nicolas Poussin, Berenger Sauniere and also Sir William St Clair at Rosslyn Chapel ... *according to the evidence.* ... In St Nazaire Et Celse the signs point to someone in recent times having knowledge of the location of the treasure. Whether it was by chance or as a result of studying the clues in St Mary Magdalene is not known. The storm damage at St

Mary Magdalene revealed to Sauniere the whereabouts of the treasure. The flood damage at Rennes les Bains in 1992 might in its turn have revealed something that led to the secret of Dagobert's gold, but other clues in St Nazaire Et Celse suggest they predate the flood damage.

The Pictures, Statues and the rest of Sauniere's work in the church of St. Mary Magdalene will one day be removed and the church restored to its rightful place in the community as a true place of worship. No doubt some of the icons will be renovated and housed in a small museum. What is certain is that the name of Berenger Sauniere and his treasure will pass into the history books and be romantically recounted in the centuries to come as one of the, *greatest treasure stories of all time.*

The treasure no longer belongs to Abbe Boudet or Berenger Sauniere, any more than it was once the property of the Cardinal or Nicolas Poussin; nor does the author of this work lay claim to it. The mystery was a challenge, which required a solution. - *'It was not the finding of the pot of gold at the end of the Rainbow that was the goal, rather it was to find the End of the Rainbow'.*

CHAPTER 16
THE END OF THE RAINBOW.

Berenger Sauniere had created a problem for himself that ultimately led to his downfall. With the Abbe Boudet's blessing he could have quietly removed enough of the treasure from St Nazaire Et Celse and secreted it elsewhere, returning from time to time to his cache to replenish his funds. Instead he became greedy and threw his money and gold around embarking on a lavish lifestyle. The whole area knew the priest had found a treasure. He projected himself as a benevolent spender enjoying the privileges of wealth and committing large sums of money to various projects. At today's values he spent two million pounds Sterling. The bulk of this money did not come from gold alone. The priest had discovered more than gold and his attempt to find a way around his dilemma not only committed him to remaining a priest, but also in selling something which was beyond price in a transaction that in the end he could not hope to honour. He spent huge sums of money on buildings, high living and charitable gifts; yet when he died he had not a penny to his name ... everything belonged to his housekeeper and companion Marie Denarnaud.

The situation had got out of hand and the priest of Rennes les Bains knew that sooner or later Sauniere's ever increasing visits to St Nazaire Et Celse would attract unwanted attention. It was Sauniere's approach to the Holy Roman Emperors, which led to the breakdown of the relationship between the two priests. Sauniere had kept his dealings with Rome quiet and had not fully consulted with Boudet in the matter. When the older man realised what Sauniere was doing he refused to allow removal of the item in question. Boudet had known for years the potential value of that and other items concealed beneath his church, but dared not hint at its existence. Whatever caused the disagreement between the priests neither man openly discussed the matter or disclosed the source of their wealth.

Stanley James in his book is convinced the treasure is in a cave and set out his case to prove it. He goes as far as to make a definitive statement. Indeed, he states: -

"Many books have been published over recent years concerning Berenger Sauniere. 'The Treasure maps of Rennes-le-Chateau' is the first to publish the solution. I have witnessed to my accurate prediction of the place of the cave from the pictures in the church. I have witnesses to my finding the exact spot. I have witnesses - deliberately necessary - of all my visits and witnesses that I found nothing in the cave at any time, except stones and bones and that I only came out with cuts, bruises, scratches, grazes, bloodied, pained and tired" – James had not discovered the cave that holds the Treasure of Rennes-le-Chateau.

In reading Sauniere's Stations of the Cross James suggests there was writing on the walls of the cave that may be attributed to the Knights Templar. However, he does not mention this in association with the cave he discovered.

We return to St Mary Magdalene and Sauniere's pictures in the Stations of the Cross. It becomes clear that the pictures may be divided into two main classes. There are those that are directional and others that offer a detailed insight into the whereabouts of the treasure.

STATION '111' Figure 16-1

In the latter group we find Stations '1', '11', '111' and 'X1V'. The scene in these four pictures is set on a floor slab and is within a building. The sequence for these pictures is shown as, Station '111', being our step eleven; Station '11' as step twelve, Station '1' is step thirteen and finally Station 'X1V'.

In Station '111' an important change has taken place. We are no longer in the countryside, although the background to the picture would suggest it. Sauniere has introduced a *floor sla*b on which the characters are standing. We are in a building and Jesus is being persuaded to stand up; Simon Cyrene is attempting to lift the cross. Behind and around the cross are soldiers with one blowing a trumpet, which is heralding our approach. We are *within sight* of the treasure. Sauniere had reached the point where if he was serious about showing the way to the treasure, yet guarded in his disclosers, he could not give too much away. He had committed himself to following Poussin's symbol on Parchment One and once this is understood by the treasure-seeker much of Sauniere's artistry becomes irrelevant. Indeed, the connection between Sauniere's pictures and Poussin's involvement with the treasure has, until now, never been properly explored. Either side of the fallen figure of Jesus (the treasure seeker) in Station '111', two characters are looking down at each other's feet, which mark the ends of the floor slab. The treasure is below the floor beneath the church of St Nazaire Et Celse.

STATION '11'   Figure 16-2

Station '11' is step twelve. In this picture Jesus is once more on His feet and carrying the cross. The Biblical placing of the station comes after Pilate condemned Jesus and allowed Him to be scourged and crowned with thorns. On the left of the picture a soldier walks ahead of Christ with his arm held high.

Here again the characters are on a floor slab. The leading person is looking down behind him, his hand pulling the hem of his tunic to one side enabling him to see what the stooping figure of Simon Cyrene is doing at the feet of Jesus. He is picking something up; a coin or similar gold object is in his right hand. Beneath Simon's left leg (in original picture) is what looks like a golden skull. One is to pick up something up after the skull, from below the feet of Jesus – below St Nazaire Et Celse.

STATION '1' Figure 16-3

The other figures around Jesus are also looking down; the right hand character has his hand on the shoulder of Jesus, *the treasure-seeker,* urging him to go on. Jesus' head is at the centre of the cross, and we are close to the *place of the treasure.*

In Station '1' there are five characters. From left to right, a Roman Centurion, Jesus, a Cleric, Pontius Pilate and a Negro boy. The Centurion stands behind Christ with his right hand resting on His shoulder, as if pushing him towards Pilate. Jesus is at the foot of the stepped dais looking down at the bowl of water held by the boy. The Centurion is also 'looking down at the water'. The Cleric or priest at the back of the group is facing the north west and looking beyond Jesus and the Soldier, in the direction of St Mary Magdalene – a gesture to Sauniere perhaps. In one hand he holds a piece of gold high above his head, in the other a napkin or vestment. Pilate is seated and looking intently down at Jesus whilst washing his hands in the bowl. One of Pilate's feet touches the lower part of Christ's garment. A curtain, which represents the *Veil of the Jerusalem Temple,* forms the backdrop, beyond which it is *Only for the Priesthood.*

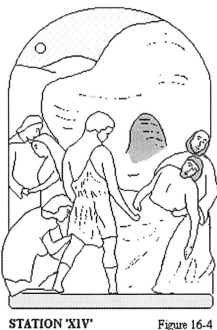

STATION 'XlV'   Figure 16-4

The Station 'XlV' picture is not easily read. In theory one might expect it to hold the last and final clue to the treasure, the climax of the quest. It is a picture of the limp body of Jesus being carried to the Tomb by Nicodemus and Joseph of Aramathea; the disconsolate women are standing to one side, with one of them at the feet of Jesus. It is a sombre picture, a darkened sky yet with a full moon and a towering black rock with the outline of a cave. The scene is outside a cave at night, yet once again the characters are all standing on a floor slab. Jesus' left arm is hanging with fingers pointing downwards; the character with his back to us is indicating the same spot. Like all puzzles the picture is never complete until the last piece is in place; there is no mistaking the clues and we are close to the treasure.

Marie Denarnaud was mistaken; the Treasure of Rennes-le-Chateau is far from where she thought it to be. The Abbe Sauniere appearing to bring the gold and large sums of money from his Church confused her. Marie's naivety had suited Sauniere's purpose well.

Similarly the Abbe Boudet who knew the source of Sauniere's wealth and his own kept the secret to himself. The old priest had enjoyed a comfortable lifestyle, occasionally helping himself to the treasure we now know as Dagobert's gold and which he was only obliged to share with Sauniere after the younger man's opportune discovery.

What we have at St. Mary Magdalene is the picture story of how to find the treasure. The secret that had once belonged to the Cardinals and Nicolas Poussin, the Abbe Boudet from 1665 to 1891 also became Berenger Sauniere's; it has remained his secret for a hundred years, despite numerous would-be pretenders to the throne. Sauniere's *works of art* in St. Mary Magdalene are nearing the end of their sustainable life and if no attempt is made at renovation then once individual items have to be removed, they might as well all be taken away. It could be a case of solving the problem whilst the clues remain, or not at all, although of course sufficient recorded information now exists on the subject to ensure that even if Sauniere's plaster and paint was no more it would make little difference to the story.

Having committed him to telling us where the treasure may be found Sauniere was at pains to spread the last few vital bits of information as thinly as possible. His artistry is clever in that there is all the pretence of the end of the trail being in the open, when in fact it is in a building. Sauniere's artwork at St Mary Magdalene was promoted by his finding of the treasure based on the discovery he made by following the clues left to us by Nicolas Poussin – just as the author of this work has done.

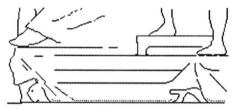

Figure 16-5

It is possible that during the past hundred years Dagobert's gold has been secretly removed and all traces of where is once lay are gone. However to remove the menorah in recent times would have attracted attention. One hundred years ago reports circulated in the villager of Rennes-le-Chateau that Marie Denarnaud was wearing ancient rings that were a present from her Pastor; others received gold coins from him. Marie was convinced the priest had discovered great wealth, enough to *keep the villagers in luxury for a hundred years*. Sauniere told no one where the treasure was located, not even Marie.

It is surprising that the Church of Rome and in particular the Bishops of Carcassonne have allowed something they deplore to continue beyond Sauniere to this day. ... If the Official position of the Church is, *"We do not believe in the existence of the Treasure "*. ... And, *"People have gone on about it and made up absurd stories "* ... why not make an end of it

119

and give back the Church of St Mary Magdalene to its parishioners for the true worship of God.

My quest for the Treasure of Rennes-le-Chateau came about as a result of seeing Henry Lincoln's compelling tales in the Chronicle Programmes and in his book, 'The Holy Place'. – The dream was that one day I would solve the mystery ... nothing else.

It is not the finding of the pot of gold at the end of the rainbow that promised the greatest reward ... it was finding the End of the Rainbow.

HIDDEN MEANINGS

Chapter 17
The Headstone
and Grave Slab

Writers on the subject of the Treasure seem convinced the secret lies in the cipher that is thought concealed in the Parchments and in the epitaph of the so-called 'headstone' associated with Marie de Negri d'Ables Dame D'Hautpoul De Blanchefort

The *headstone* inscription is used to provide the 'key words' linked to the codes and ciphers which are attributed by some to the Abbe Antoine Bigou, who was the Parish priest around the time of the Noble Lady Hautpoul's demise.

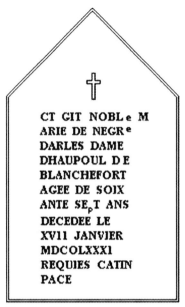

CT GIT NOBL e M
ARIE DE NEGR e
DARLES DAME
DHAUPOUL D E
BLANCHEFORT
AGEE DE SOIX
ANTE SE p T ANS
DECEDEE LE
XVll JANVIER
MDCOLXXXl
REQUIES CATIN
PACE

Sketch of Headstone   Figure 17-1

The Grave Slab, which supposedly formed part of the Noble Lady's grave furniture and of which only Sauniere's sketch remains, was believed defaced and left smashed by him and left in the churchyard.

The translated inscription on the Headstone reads: -

'HERE LIES THE NOBLE MARIE DE NEGRI D'ABLES DAME D'HAUTPOUL

De BLANCHEFORT AGED SIXTY SEVEN YEARS DIED THE SEVENTEENTH JANUARY 1781 MAY SHE REST IN PEACE'.

The Headstone and the Grave Slab is the subject of a controversy that has proven to be a stumbling block to finding the treasure. Neither Berenger Sauniere nor the author of this work, or for that matter the Abbe Gelis, required the ciphers or the headstone to locate the treasure. The ciphers are and always have been either a cleverly contrived prank or a serious attempt by an individual or number of individuals to frustrate the treasure seeker.

A reproduction of the *headstone* is in the Presbytery Museum. It is a fake and a misrepresentation, which if the original stone existed at all it could only have done so in that form with the Noble Ladies daughters consent. Henry Lincoln has commented that the word 'Catin', within the epitaph, was, *"An extraordinary error to find inscribed on the tomb of a Noble Lady"*. We might also question that the Abbe Bigou would have consented to a headstone with that inscription to be placed in a consecrated churchyard. There is also the problem of the construction or alteration of the Altar and the composition of the Parchments. The Noble lady had died in 1781 with her estate in need of funds. She had already disposed of lands to meet her needs and it is therefore unlikely if the headstone and the codes were design to conceal accessible family treasures that could not have amounted to a great deal and hardly worth going to great lengths to conceal it. If on the other hand the codes refer to other than that belonging to the Noble lady what was the point of involving her. France was in a state of political unrest that led to the Revolution of 1789. Life for the clergy as well as the nobility became very insecure and along with his Bishop Bigou made his way across the border into Spain, where he died a few years later. Although there was a period of eight or nine years between the death of the Noble lady and Bigou's departure – time enough one might think for the Abbe to achieve all that he is credited with – it probably was his intention that once the uproar had died down he would return to resume his duties at Rennes-le-Chateau. There was no requirement to plant an unusual headstone that would have attracted unnecessary attention.

It is demonstrated that it was Nicolas Poussin who wrote the Parchments, something that whoever concocted the ciphers either did not realise, or deliberately avoided mentioning. The Blanchefort family or other treasure appears to have been used to provide a smoke screen to conceal the whereabouts of Dagobert's gold. Those who wrote the ciphers have manipulated the excess letters in Parchment Two and added a fictitious headstone to create an unsolvable cipher.

The Parchments and the slab both include a symbol in the form of a looped (P-S), but it is the uncharacteristic letters 'MORTepee' lifted from the headstone that are used as the key to the cipher, when one imagines that if a cipher existed at all, including the key, it should be set out in the Parchments.

The message said to emerge from the cipher and based on use of the Tableau de Vigenere system; here translated into English it apparently reads: -

'SHEPERDESS NO TEMPTATION THAT POUSSIN TENIERS HOLD THE KEY PEACE 681 BY THE CROSS AND THE HORSE OF GOD I COMPLETE THIS DAEMON GUARDIAN AT MIDDAY BLUE APPLES'.

After reading the book by Gérard de Sède entitled 'Le Trésor Maudit', Henry Lincoln recounts how he received from de Sède a decipherment of the codes based on the Vigenere system, using the headstone letters. It is further reported that a Pierre Plantard de St Clair, associated with the secret society of the Priory of Sion, said the parchments were 'cooked up in the

1950's by a man called Philippe de Cherisey', who was present when the statement was made and who later suggested the parchments were based on very good originals.

A number of years ago BBC 2 Horizon broadcast a programme entitled, 'The History of a Mystery', that featured the book by Andrews and Schellenberger entitled, 'The Tomb of God'. In the BBC film Gérard de Sède is reported as saying, "He had found his explanation for the mystery in the Bibliotheque Nationale in Paris, where someone had deposited a curious collection of typescript and photocopies called, *The Secret Dossier*". This dossier, never authenticated by the library, was written under a pseudonym. It contained genealogies of a quasi-Masonic charter and sketches of an Aristocrat's tomb, which Sauniere is said to have dug up. This led de Sède to his most exciting discovery; two parchments that purported to be the ones found by Sauniere's bell ringer. What is more, they contained secret messages written in code. Gérard de Sède went on to say that when he submitted the cryptographic document he had found to the Cipher Office they confirmed the documents were encoded. However, he also says, it got (us) nowhere because (we) ended up with a message that is completely nonsensical. Here we have a conflicting story that appears to discount the popular belief that Sauniere discovered the parchments in one of the Altar pillars.

Because no satisfactory conclusions may be drawn from the 'nonsensical' message, which is a meaningless jumble of words, it has led writers into blind alleys. Henry Lincoln has chosen a myriad of endless radiating lines. The Fanthorpe's have introduced theology, alchemy and overseas enigmas. Andrews and Schellenberger considered the *Tomb of Jesus* was at the heart of the matter. Many other theories abound, but none are any closer to solving the mystery. The BBC programmers brought to light inconsistencies that surround the mystery, their researchers did their homework and the *experts* had no answers. The programme makers were not about to offer a solution, their aim, if not to discredit the story, was to show the weaknesses in the arguments of those participating.

The additional 140 letters that accompany the text on Parchment Two are taken from of St. John's Gospel Chapter X11, verses 1 to 11. They include the recognisable twelve letters forming the words, 'AD GENESARETH' and leave 64 letters: -

VCPSJ QRO VYMYYDLT PohRBOXT ODJLBKNJ
FQUEPAJY NPPBFEIE LRGHIIRY BTTCVxGD.
above, with a further 64 letters below 'AD GENESARETH' -
LUCCVMTE JHPNPGSV QJHGMLFT SVJLZQMT
OXANPEMU PHKORPKH VJCMCATL VQXGGNDT

Poussin's intention is unclear, but it could point to a chessboard configuration suggesting a simple cipher along the lines of the Tableau de Vigenere. However, the painter may also have known of the 'Caesar Cipher', used by Julius Caesar. There is also a cipher that uses a chessboard knight to track every square on the board and in the extreme may produce a coded message. Whatever the reason for the letters, they are not required for the purposes of locating Dagobert's gold.

Gérard de Sède, Lincoln and others have used the letters 'MORTepee' lifted from the headstone as the Key words. Fanthorpe has tried using 'Sauniere', but clearly as it was Poussin who wrote the parchments that predated Marie de Negre d'Ables he could not have visualised her headstone.

The Headstone has to be regarded as a hoax and we should concentrate instead on the Grave Slab, as it is the work of Nicolas Poussin. Indeed it is easier to prove the case than not. Lincoln, Fanthorpe nor James offer evidence that Bigou or anyone else associated with the so-called ciphers had any idea of the whereabouts of Dagobert's treasure or are able to link it with what Berenger Sauniere is said to have discovered buried under the floor of his church. In the BBC film Gérard de Sède confirms he saw what was discovered under the *Knights Tombstone* in the church and that it amounted to very little; hardly warranting the involvement of unwieldy and complicated codes to conceal it.

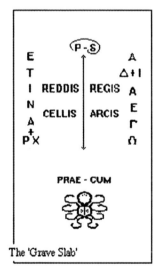

Figure 17-2

The slab discovered by Sauniere under the church floor dates from the Knights Templar and is twelfth century. That does not rule out its reuse at a later date, but it clearly places it much later than the Visigoth period. The key to its origin lies in the newel or pulpit post, which is preserved in the cavern museum at the Villa Bethanie. That post contained a secret compartment, which was discovered by Sauniere's bell ringer. The compartment held a small glass phial and within it a parchment note. It would be interesting to have the timber in the post dated (dendrochronology) that should establish the age of the message *in the bottle*. The items discovered under the slab may prove to have a symbolic rather than material value.

Whoever was responsible for the ciphers failed to take into account details that should not have been overlooked had they known the whole story. One senses a conspiracy with someone in authority being behind the plot; someone who might state, *"There wasn't any treasure at Rennes-le-Chateau and the Abbot Sauniere neither had to look for it or find it*!"

The stone referred to as the *Grave slab* has both Latin and Greek inscriptions on it. It was created by Nicolas Poussin around 1640; and not used as external grave furniture. One hundred and thirty years of weathering would have seriously eroded the inscription long before anyone attempted to sketch it. More than that, its apparent mystery could have attracted undue attention and vandalism; it was far safer inside St. Mary Magdalene.

The *grave slab* is not the same as the *Knight's Tombstone* and because of the slab's close links with the parchments and the painting it suggest it is 'Poussin' in origin and therefore dates from around 1646 AD. Its fate is unknown, but once again if it is true the priest destroyed it he took the trouble to sketch it first.

The looped P-S symbol on the slab identifies it with the Parchments and the letters 'Et In' also with Poussin's painting *Les Berger's d'Arcadie*. With the looped letters pointing to the French word 'OR' for gold and the Latin words REDDIS REGIS CELLIS ARCIS on the slab meaning, *'The Gold at Royal Reddis is in the Storerooms below the Fortress',* which when taken together with 'Prae-Cum' and the *spider* (menorah) we have a statement that might read - *'The Gold at Royal Reddis is in the Storerooms below the Fortress together with the Menorah"*; the double-headed Arrow on the slab providing a link.

There appear to be a number of distinct messages on the slab. The one tells us of, *'The Gold at Royal Reddis'* that relates to the *Treasure of Rennes-le-Chateau,* with a second message in the upper part of the left hand column, which Lincoln points out might mean ... 'Et In Arc' (and in Arc). We then have the symbol of a cross (+) that we first saw in Parchment One and which was used to separate text.

According to Stanley James there is a difficulty in that the last three letters in the left hand column on the slab, are Greek letters. The letter 'A' is placed above the '+', the 'P' and the 'X' below. The Latin 'ET IN' together with the Greek 'A' may still be taken to read 'And in Arcadia', as Lincoln suggests.

The word 'ARCADIA' in *Les Berger's d'Arcadie* is also used by Poussin to direct us to Arques. It is a puzzle why the painter should resort to using Greek letters on the Slab when it seems the message he had conveyed in Latin was adequate for the purpose. He may have used the change of language to draw attention to the *Chatsworth* painting and in particular the River God Alpheius, the River Alpheius and its tributaries flowed through Arcadia in ancient Greece. That river is likened by the locals as akin the river Rialscssc – the river of the Kings Gold – which flows through Arques.

Poussin's emphasis is placed on Arcadia of which the *Grave slab* forms an integral part. He designed it as an insurance policy against the possible loss of the paintings. In the event the paintings have survived although in the Art world their true significance has not been acknowledged. Under normal circumstances the slab would out live the paintings, but thanks to the intervention of the priest Sauniere circumstances have change dramatically.

Early Greek	A 𝛿 1 Δ � 𝟶 1 B 𝟸 𝟸 𝟷 1 𝑀 𝟶 O 1 Φ 𝟷 𝟻 X Y Y Y 𝟮 ... I
Classical Greek	A B Γ Δ E Γ H I I K Λ M N O Π . P Σ T Y Y Y Ξ Z
Etruscan	A 𝟹 1 𝑑 𝟶 𝟹 𝟷 B I I X 𝟷 M H O 1 P 𝟺 𝟹 T Y Y 𝟷 X 𝟸
Early Latin	A B < D E F < H I I K ⊦ M N O Γ Q P 𝟸 T V V V X Y Z
Classical Latin	A B C D E F G H I I K L M N O P Q R S T V V V X Y Z
Modern Roman	A B C D E F G H I J K L M N O P Q R S T U V W X Y Z

Reference made to Collins English Dictionary and Thesaurus

Figure 17-3

After the cross in the left hand column the remaining letters, including those in the right hand column are Greek. – It is at this point my crude attempt at unravelling the meaning of the slab letters may be called into question – none the less, I propose the following.

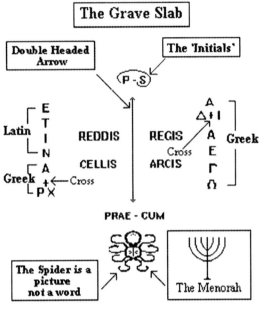

Figure 17-4

After 'And in Arcadia', and, if it is the case we are dealing with a number of statements separated by crosses then the second part comprises ... 'PXA Δ' (delta) where from the table we find the Greek 'P' becomes the Classical Latin 'R'. The Early Greek 'X' may read as a 'T'; the 'A' stands as 'A' and 'Δ' is the Latin 'D', resulting 'R T A D'. However, it better suits my purposes if we read the rearranged letters as 'RXAD'. The 'R' is assumed to mean Rennes; the 'X' is the Roman/Christian cross, signifying 'Church' and the 'AD' as Latin means 'to' or 'towards'. This allows me to read the statement as ... 'To (the) Church (at) Rennes'.

The last set of Greek letters after the second cross (+) is, 'I A E r Ω', which may be read as... 'I A E G O' or, 'I A EGO'. Where the 'I' is the Standing Stone, the 'A' is *by* or *from* ... and it reads ... 'I (am) by (the) Standing Stone'.

The three statements, taken in the order found give us ... 'And in Arques' + 'To (the) Church (at) Rennes' + 'I from (the) Standing Stone'. In other words we have the completed message reading: -

'From the Standing Stone at Arques (go) to the Church at Rennes'.

[The Standing Stone is discussed in a later chapter.]

The message on the slab appears as a confusing direction indicator. The centre section sends us to *the Fortress* at Rennes les Bains and the columns of letters direct us back from Arques to Rennes-le-Chateau - the complete opposite to both the *Louvre* and the *Chatsworth* that point us to Arques.

Such a message would be an amazing statement to find on anyone's *Grave Slab* without a very specific reason for doing so. In this case if indeed the slab was part of the Noble Lady's grave furniture one should have expected it to play an important part in the scheme of things. Apparently not, whoever decided to *take the Noble Lady's name in vain,* did not have the courtesy to have a closer look at the so-called *Grave Slab.* I feel it is correct to assume that the only purpose for the codes was to place a stumbling block in the path of the treasure seeker. To that end it has been most successful. There is now no doubt the ciphers are post Sauniere and a worthless distraction.

The message on the Slab was immensely valuable. It informs us, *The Gold at Royal Reddis is in the Storerooms below the Fortress together with the Menorah'*. It directs us to Arques, *'And in Arques'* and then redirects us from Arques, back to the *Church at Rennes'*. It might appear odd that Poussin should place the slab with its dual directional messages at Rennes-le-Chateau when on the one hand it points us to Dagobert's gold at Rennes les Bains and on the other to Arques. Presumably it was done to keep the clues together in one safe place

The Grave slab was not a fake nor was it the grave furniture associated with Marie de Negri d'Ables Dame D'Hautpoul De Blanchefort. Sauniere well understood this and probably realised the columns of letters related to other than *his treasure,* yet he may not have noticed that *Les Berger's d'Arcadie* was also directing him to Arques ... besides, he had enough to be going on with and perhaps when the situation became so desperate for him it was too late to do anything about it.

Furthermore and fortunately for us, if indeed he had destroyed the evidence of the Slab in a way it backfired, for in preserving a sketch of the slab he *preserved* the slab. It might be the case that the slab still exists and could once again be forming part of an Altar, Sauniere's Altar! ... Like Poussin it seems that his intention was that knowledge of the treasure should not be entirely lost and that as well as preserving the Altar pillar the slab too might still be at Mary Magdalene.

If the extra 128 letters in Parchment Two do constitute the basis of a Cipher and it is ever decoded it may provide a link with the second message and support my theory that there is a *Treasure of Arques.* The *Grave slab* was Poussin's insurance for the project and has an importance that is both revealing and exciting. The purpose for all the expense and elaborate clues was that someday; *'in the centuries to come'* someone in authority would be able to find the treasure and not only Dagobert's gold. For this purpose the Slab needed to be kept in a good state of preservation and where better than as the *Tabletop to an Altar.*

If Stanley James is correct in his reading of Sauniere, amongst the treasure in St Nazaire Et Celse was the seven stemmed candlestick or Menorah that had been part of the Temple Artefacts taken from Jerusalem by the Romans. The candlestick was of pure gold of beaten work. It had seven arms, the centre one being above the shaft, formed on each side of three cups of almond blossoms, their knops and flowers. The design of the menorah and its base is thought to be as depicted on the Arch of Titus in Rome. There were separate lamps, which were placed on the top of the seven branches, each being detachable from the candlestick itself. The lamps were supplied with oil from vessels some of which may also be amongst the treasure. The overall size of the candlestick can only be guessed at, perhaps comfortable working height for hanging the lamps - say 4'6". Its weight is thought to be about 150 lbs. The lamps were lit and trimmed daily by the priests and kept constantly burning. There were Tongs and snuff dishes - the whole candlestick, lamps, oil vessels, tongs and snuff dishes made from one talent of pure gold. - One talent is equal to 158 lbs.

The *Louvre* and *Chatsworth* pictures were intended to be complete at the same time and to form a composite plan for the concealment of the treasures and both like the slab held the same message ... Et In Arcadia Ego.

CHAPTER 18
ET IN ARCADIA EGO

Every serious student of the Treasure of Rennes-le-Chateau becomes familiar with the words 'Et In Arcadia Ego'. The phrase is central to Poussin's painting *Les Berger's d'Arcadie*, the Parchments and the *Grave slab*. ... *Et In Arcadia Ego* means ... well, what exactly does it mean.

Because of the association with a skull and tomb, particularly in the earlier painting by *Guercino* and the *Chatsworth* version of the Arcadian Shepherds by Poussin, the general interpretation of the words is taken to mean, *though I am now dead I was once in Arcadia*. However, the *Guercino* and the *Chatsworth* are not seen in the same relation to the treasure as the *Louvre*; in that picture there is no skull.

The Arcadian Shepherds
by Guercino

Figure 18-1

Not being a classical Latin scholar one might be excused for resorting to the use of a standard Latin dictionary in a crude attempt to resolve the problem. ... 'Et' may be read as *also*; 'In' as *In*; Arcadia as it is written and 'Ego' as *I*. ... Roughly translated as, 'I (was) also in Arcadia'. ... Latin scholars may not be amused.

Arcadia was a mountainous area in central Peloponneus in ancient Greece, known today as Arkadhia. It was a plateau bounded on the north and east by ranges of hills and mountains. The western plateau is open with some mountains through which the River Alpheius and its tributaries flow. It was an isolated area, virtually cut off from the mainland on all sides and its isolation partially explains why it was considered a paradise both by Greek and Roman poets and later in Renaissance literature. In Poussin's *Chatsworth* painting he is said to depict an idyllic setting for *pastoral poetry and scene of simple pleasure*. The shepherds are with a lovely female companion walking in the land of Arcadia and come across an imposing tomb. In dreamy contemplation they run their fingers across the letters ... *Et In Arcadia Ego* ... Yet, even in Arcadia death makes its presence felt. ... That more or less is the interpretation put upon Poussin's painting by those who study the masterpiece and advise us as to how we should view the painting. The reality is somewhat different.

However the inscription *Et In Arcadia Ego* in the painting of the *Tomb of Arques* is interpreted in the Art World and whether or not the experts' distance themselves and the paintings from the mystery, evidence in this work unveils the painting's true secrets. Blunt was wrong, but it remains to be seen if Lincoln and the writer of this work agree after further revelations in the picture. Those who hold the view that there is more to *Les Berger's d'Arcadie* than meets the eye are in distinguished company, for Louis XIV of France acquired the painting in the firm belief and with first hand knowledge that it did hold a secret to immense wealth.

Choosing the site for the tomb was not something to be done in a hurry or with a casual glance along the road. Henry Lincoln has shown a vista looking out over the tomb from higher ground on the north side of the road and picks out the salient points, just as Poussin did in his painting.

The location of the *Tomb of Arques* is not within the immediate vicinity of the village of Arques; it is about one kilometre west at the small hamlet of Pontils. From the road bridge over the stream one looks across the ravine up to the rocky outcrop where the remains of the base can still be seen. In 1988 the owner of the land demolished the tomb after repeated attempts by trespassers to find the treasure. Lincoln and others who have visited the site of the tomb and compared the landscape with the background in Poussin's painting are persuaded the painter had been at Pontils; and if at Pontils then, *'I was also in Arcadia'*, or as I am proposing ... *'I was also in Arques'*.

It is said that Nicolas Poussin took his visual source for the composition of both the *Chatsworth* and the *Louvre* versions of the Arcadian Shepherds from the earlier painting by the Bolognese painter Guercino. The same brief was given to both painters, but it was Poussin who developed the theme of *Et In Arcadia Ego,* first in the *Chatsworth* around 1627 and later in the *Louvre* c.1638. The phrase came ready-made from the Cardinals, and it meant Arques.

It becomes clear that Nicolas Poussin probably visited the locality around Arques on more than one occasion and became familiar with the countryside. This enabled him to show important and recognisable detail in his work. Poussin had left Paris for Rome around 1623 - 1624, returning to his native France for a two-year period from October 1640 to September 1642. There is no record of his making other visits, which is why art historians, even though they are at a loss to offer an explanation for the setting of the *Tomb of Arques,* refuse to acknowledge it as his handiwork.

Around the time of painting the *Chatsworth* Poussin was extremely busy, in fact he gave as his reason for postponing the visit to Paris as pressure of work. It is probable that the *Louvre* was at least in sketch form as early as 1627 and it will be shown that a feature of that picture indicates it is consistent with an early visit to the region. There is no disputing the *Tomb of Arques* existed; there are photographs and witnesses. The argument that the edifice was designed and built to 'mirror' the *Louvre* Tomb is without foundation, the site of the Tomb was carefully chosen by the painter.

By comparison the *Guercino* was a studio work and lacked the 'hands-on' detail of Poussin's painting. It was imprecise and inadequate for the purpose required. We note the tomb, skull, two shepherds and water in the *Guercino,* but that is all. It is not capable of being interpreted in the same way as the *Louvre* or the *Chatsworth* and it offers no association with Rennes-le Chateau or Arques.

The brief given to both Guercino and Poussin for the early paintings was quite specific. Whether at that time the painters were told of the real purpose of the work they were asked to undertake is not known. It would be understandable that when the idea of committing the secret to other than by word of mouth the Cardinals were guarded in just how much information they were prepared to release. That would perhaps account for the nondescript painting by Guercino. Much later, having thought about the problem the Cardinals, after having made acquaintance with Poussin, decided he was a painter with a greater eye for detail.

The Barberini knew of Dagobert's gold as well as what I am describing as, the *Treasure of Arques.* In deed, we are directed first and foremost to Arques and left in no doubt that it is the place to be. It is the subject of the inscription on the tombs and the evidence points to the second treasure being of greater importance than that of Dagobert's gold. Precisely how important may never be determined because whereas we know something of the extent of the treasure under St Nazaire Et Celse, from sources such as Poussin, Sauniere and Stanley James, we have no idea what is concealed at Arques. This may help to explain why the Holy Roman Emperors did a deal with Sauniere, they could not be sure of his source for whatever was on offer.

Poussin's sketches had impressed the Barberini; he was perceived to be a trustworthy man given to methodical and imaginative work. It was decided that he should be given as much information as possible to aid his commission. Inevitably of course this ran the risk of committing the Holy Men to releasing the whole story and a study of the Arcadian Shepherd pictures draws one to conclude Poussin did know all there was to know of the treasures, enabling him to produce cleverly crafted pictures. Undoubtedly knowledge of so much treasure whetted the painter's appetite for the 'taste' of gold - not uncommon in any man ... witness the interest today in the *Treasure of Rennes-le-Chateau.* Poussin was no fool and his enthusiasm, honesty and integrity was well rewarded with commissions for his work. None the less, eventually knowledge that *Les Berger's d'Arcadie* contained the secret of immense wealth did leak out and one source was undoubtedly Poussin.

The secret of the treasures was known by the Church of Rome from the 13th and 14th centuries and handed down through a succession of Cardinals and Popes. Francesco Barberini became a Pontificate Cardinal in 1623 when twenty-six years of age; his uncle was Pope Urban V111 at a time when a new era was in full swing and Rome was being transformed into a vast building site. Things were being set in order and it was considered that the secrets of the treasures would be better recorded than further passed on by word of mouth or even entirely forgotten.

Poussin had come to the attention of the Barberini after a successful commission to design one of the Altars in St. Peter's. The Frenchman, eager to gain the patronage of this important family could hardly have believed what he was being asked to undertake. It would not have been easy for the Barberini who were about to impart to a stranger a secret of immense wealth that had been closely guarded for the past two hundred and fifty years. Men of Holy Orders, from a line of those who during their lives were privy to many secrets through the confessional were taking what some would consider as an irrational and unethical step. The Barberini knew that knowledge of the treasure did not automatically offer rights of possession, a fact that quickly became apparent to the painter. The secret had become a burden and the family could see no obvious successor within the Church of Rome. They sought the help of someone they felt confidant would respect the trust placed in him.

When Poussin's work was complete and the paintings safely in the hands of the Cardinals they must have felt their secret was sealed forever. However, dispersal of the paintings particularly *Les Berger's d'Arcadie* later aroused concern and undoubtedly resulted in the memorial to the painter two hundred years after his death.

The arrival of Sauniere on the scene sent shock waves through the system and caused consternation within the Church. It stirred the depths of vague memories of those in authority who at that time had recollections of ancient treasures with which the Church was associated. The key to the secret had long been mislaid the or even lost forever and no one had any idea of what was involved. Both Boudet and Sauniere would have discussed the treasure in detail and been fully aware of its history. They would also have concluded that the Church of Rome in times past knew of the hoard. In Rome the Church was getting its act together and was anxious to learn how the priest discovered the treasure; more to the point, which treasure was it. They may have reasoned that what comprised Dagobert's treasure held little interest, but if it was the Cathar hoard that would be a different matter altogether. However, at the time of Sauniere's approach with the particular item it seems the Church did not know the location of either treasure.

Since the 1970's the quest has always been to discover the *Treasure of Rennes-le-Chateau*, yet Poussin and the Cardinal's of the day principal occupation appeared to be with the *Treasure of Arques*. The earlier *Chatsworth* painting had set the scene, later supported by the *Louvre*, with both pointing to Arques.

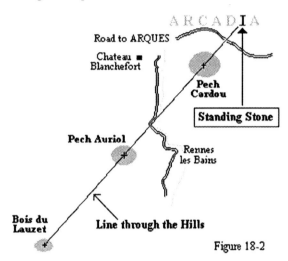

Figure 18-2

When my Figure 18-2 was being drawn from the map it led to an interesting find. The line through the three hills, Bois du Lauzet, Auriol and beyond the high peak Cardou, when extended across the road to Arques precisely met the Pierre Dressee or Standing Stone. [*Previously referred to*]. At first it was looked upon as no more than a coincidence, but when taken in context with the *Chatsworth* painting that *coincidence* took on a whole new meaning. It was seen that once again the heads of the female and the two shepherds were also in a line and furthermore the second shepherd's finger was this time pointing not at the letter 'R' but directly at the letter 'I' in Arcadia.

The search for Dagobert's gold has only acknowledged *Les Berger's d'Arcadie,* principally through Henry Lincoln's use of it as the basis for his pentagon drawing. The *Chatsworth,* although known to exist, has had no role to play in the search. However, it can be seen that in the *Louvre* and in the *Chatsworth,* the heads of the shepherds and female are in a straight line.

Ten years elapsed between the completion of the *Chatsworth* and the *Louvre.* Time enough for the painter to reflect on and develop his strategy to cross reference the later picture and begin his plans for the Parchments and the Grave Slab. The complete undertaking took the painter many years to finish. The more one understands Poussin's involvement the more amazed one becomes over the enormity of the task. It was not only the *Chatsworth* and the *Louvre* he had to complete, there were also a number of others paintings that will be dealt with later. It was a lifetime's work, from 1626 when Poussin first visited Arques to the building of the Altar at Mary Magdalene and the concealing of the Parchments.

The Louvre together with the Parchments and the *Grave slab* directed us to St. Nazaire Et Celse at Rennes les Bains. It was only the chance discovery of the line through the hills to the stone that set the writer on the course for Arques. Poussin not only used the 'R' and the 'C' in the word Arcadia to indicate Rennes-le Chateau, he also, through the word, directs us to Arques.

The word ARCADIA, when split it into its component parts, reads ... **A** (in Latin) meaning '*from*' or *after*; the R and **C** we have determined as '*Rennes-le-Chateau*'; AD means '*to*', the I is for the '*Standing Stone*', with the last letter **A** taken to represent '*Arques*'... The message then reads: -

From Rennes-le-Chateau (go) to (the) Standing Stone (at) Arques.

Figure 18-3

This is consistent with the direction given by the line through the hills to the Standing Stone; it also corresponds with the line through the heads in the *Chatsworth*, which highlights the letter 'I' as the Standing Stone. It was beginning to look as though the two pictures were more closely interwoven than was at first thought and entirely possible the *Louvre* was in detail sketch form ten years before it was finally completed. It was an instant hit following Poussin's revelation to the Abbe Fouquet that it held a great secret and became sought after, particularly around 1685, when it eventually entered the collection of the court of Louis X1V of France, who locked it away.

The fate of the *Chatsworth* is less well known; it was first mentioned in 1677 in the inventory drawn up after the death of Cardinal Camillo Massimi, where it is paired with '*Midas washing himself at the source of the Pactolus*'.

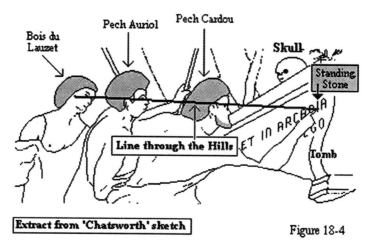

Figure 18-4

Treasure seekers have never taken the *Louvre* seriously. In the main they have accepted Henry Lincoln's geometry of the picture, which has led nowhere. The *Chatsworth* has fared less well with some suggesting there may be hidden Christian and other symbolism in the picture, but just as for the *Louvre* they notice little that would fire the imagination. The tomb in the *Chatsworth* picture rests on a rock and parallels the Tomb of Arques that is also set on a rocky outcrop. Sauniere should have known of the Standing stone but have been unaware of the *Chatsworth,* although he knew that a second treasure was hinted at on the *Grave slab.* The earlier painting is very challenging and cleverly constructed, something that only becomes evident when the picture is more closely examined.

The location of the *Tomb of Arques,* that is the key to both pictures, required first hand knowledge of the area; purchase of the land and preparation of drawings. A local mason was contracted to construct the edifice and if Poussin was responsible for the Standing Stone, which appears likely, then that too would have required preplanning and subsequent placing around 1627; the time of the *Chatsworth* painting. It is possible the stone was in place long before Poussin arrived on the scene, but if so Guercino should have known of it. The stone was not in place at the time of Merovingian kings, nor is there evidence the Templars knew of its existence.

The stone is no lightweight, it stands almost three metres above ground line, weights in at around five metric tonnes and required a sizeable workforce to quarry, transport and place it. It could only have been sited with the aid of a fairly accurate map or the improbability of an observer climbing to the top of Cardou. Had it not been for vandals posing as treasure seekers the important *Tomb of Arques* would be in place today, but the misguided belief that treasure was hidden within the tomb has robbed future generations of an impressive landmark. ... It should be clearly stated that there is no point 'attacking' the Pierre Dressee or Standing stone for no treasure is buried under or anywhere near it.

The 'Chatsworth' Finger

Figure 18-5

The three hills had, *in their order stood* since time in memorial and were used in their natural form to provide the basis for setting out the location of the Dagobert's treasure. The Standing Stone arrived on the scene much later and was deliberately placed by Nicolas Poussin for the purpose of the Treasure of Arques.

With so much emphasis being placed on Arques - Et In Arcadia Ego, one has to wonder why. It is probable that the Church of Rome of the day had little use for the material wealth at Rennes les Bains, but a deal of interest in the Spiritual Treasure that was of the heretic Cathar at Arques. The inventory of that treasure was unknown to them, only its location. The fact that Rome paid Sauniere so much cash in advance would indicate it was for an important *Religious item* they had previously been unaware of.

The quest now is to find the ... *Treasure of Arques*.

OTHER TREASURES

CHAPTER 19
THE TREASURE OF ARQUES

The climb to the old Cathar fortress of Montsegur is a daunting prospect and not for the faint hearted. Even so for those who make the effort and succeed it is a most rewarding experience. Not just for the remarkable views from such a vantage point but also for the sense of achievement.

Knowing a little of the story of the siege it was not difficult to imagine the desperate plight of those Cathar who endured to the end in 1244. Their betrayal and awful fate that eventually befell them is remembered on the plinth at the bottom of the hill. A few weeks before Montsegur fell a few Cathar or Perfect escaped carrying with them treasures and other legacies and as legend has it, what was said to be the Holy Grail. This is supposedly the cup taken from the Last Supper and used at the crucifixion to collect blood from Jesus' wounds; it became the romantic quest of many knights.

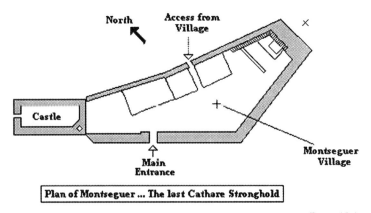

Figure 19-1

The siege lasted far longer than was anticipated. It began in the spring of 1243 and ended in March 1244. The besieging army that encamped at the foot of Montsegur lacked numbers and was unable to effectively surround the fortress. The defenders came and went much as they pleased in the early months and there was no shortage of supplies. The garrison comprised mainly of older men, women and children who had taken refuge, with around one hundred and fifty fighting men; far too many personnel for such a small place and most found crude accommodation in rough huts on any available space outside the fortress walls. They were in a good defensive position and providing supplies could reach the defenders they were well placed to resist. As the months passed and more and more besieging soldiers arrived it became evident that lines of supply to the Castle were being cut off and the inevitability of capitulation loomed. It was at this time that certain of the defenders were charged with taking from the fortress such items of gold, silver and other valuables to conceal, first on the slopes of Montsegur and later in a prearrange location away from the fortress. It is also probably that the more important items of their faith, such as scrolls or books were also removed for safekeeping.

The name Cathar comes from the Greek katharos, meaning 'pure'. They were considered by the established Church of Rome to be a heretical sect, known also as Albigensians and loosely termed Christians. The Albigensians movement was centred at Toulouse and in nearby districts rather than at ancient Albiga in southern France. The Cathar ideology showed a consistently anti-Catholic attitude with distinctive sacraments, especially the baptism of the spirit. The Cathar adopted a belief that was opposed to the orthodox view and pictured Jesus as being a rebel against the cruelty of an omnipotent God, This doctrine was anathema to Catholicism and Pope Lucius III initiated an inquisition against the Albigensians in 1184.

A more intense and sustained crusade was launched against the Cathar in 1208 under the elder Simon de Montfort. Thousands of Cathar was killed before the movement was crushed in 1244. The remaining Cathar had to go underground and although there are reports of remnants lingering on through the 14th century around Arques, they finally disappeared early in the 15th Century.

Shortly before the fall of Montsegur a small number of Cathar escaped taking with them the last remaining books so that nothing of religious significance, the Holy writings of the Cathar would fall into the hands of the Church of Rome. Once safeguarded, the hope was that the writings would enable those who survived, in due course, to re-establish the Cathar belief.

The Barberini Cardinals would not have placed so much emphasis on the whereabouts of concealed Cathar *treasure*, had it comprised only of mineral wealth. The Church of Rome considered the Cathar spiritual treasures to be of greater value than Dagobert's gold and once its location was discovered it was to remain a closely guarded secret. Yet strangely it is the clue to that very secret that is at the centre of Poussin's paintings.

The inquisition had extracted all they required to know of the heretics and ensured their treasures were under *lock and key*. Not all Cathar perished and what had been hidden would in some way have had its whereabouts noted and the signs understood by the survivors. Over time however the memory faded and it is a matter for speculation as to whether or not those signs still exist. Even if they do, without clues and some knowledge of the Languedoc it would not be possible to locate the Cathar treasure … except that is for the intervention of the Church Authorities in the guise of the Barberini family. Although we might not recognise or understand any Cathar signs, courtesy of the Cardinals we can read the clues as presented by Nicolas Poussin. The Church of Rome of the day ensured the demise of the Cathar and the secret sealing up of their religious books and treasures. Paradoxically through Poussin that secret may now be discovered.

At today's valuation any of Poussin's work is priceless. In his day the painter was slow and methodical and fees for his work reflected that cost. What lies hidden in the Languedoc area must, on that basis, be of inestimable value and the secret of its whereabouts holds the key to the Cathar belief.

The Cathar and the Templars were no fools and although under duress they had revealed the places of concealment of their treasure, it was where no individual, group or clergy could recover them and from where not even the Church of Rome would attempt to remove it. Dagobert's gold is in a church, but the whereabouts of the Cathar treasure has yet to be revealed.

The Barberini family thought that once Poussin had completed his commission their secret was secured for *centuries to come* and that there was no danger of it being rediscovered and falling into the wrong hands, thus igniting a revival in the heretic's religion. Time and fading memory should have ensured that knowledge of the treasure passed into obscurity, but the arrival of Berenger Sauniere threatened to dramatically change the situation.

The key to the Cathar secret was at first known to only a few and as the years passed it was lost completely. Today, although the key to the secret is widely recognised, as such it is not understood. It forms the central theme for some of Poussin's paintings and plays an important role in this story. The phrase chosen by the Cardinals was based on something associated with the Cathar ... I was once in Arques.

According to a register kept by a Jacques Fournier, there were still a few Cathar in and around the village of Arques for a number of years after 1244, some of who may have had knowledge of the whereabouts of the treasure and were capable of leaving durable signs that might exist to this day.

Arques is a small village that straddles the D613 road and has been in existence for centuries, perhaps as long as Rennes les Bains, which was known in Roman times. The original castle at Arques was recorded as before 1154 and the village was a Cathar centre where the historian, writer and founder of the Cathar revival Déodat Roch lived and died (1877-1978). A museum at Arques is devoted to his works. ... This must be a place to visit, as he would have known the *Tomb of Arques* well and there may be information in his museum that is revealing. Déodat Roch could have seen and met Berenger Sauniere or known of him, but what is more he probably knew where the Cathar treasures were concealed, either through folklore or a tangible sign or marker.

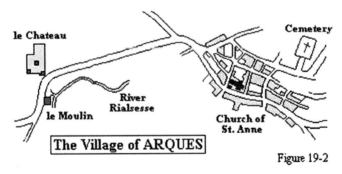

Figure 19-2

The only available layout of the Village of Arques was to the small scale of 1 to 25,000. Further information was obtained from the Syndicat D'Initiative in Rennes les Bains; the brochure was in French language only and included a map or Street Plan of the Village of Arques that set out the usual points of interest. The information on the village reveals the church tower was part of the original castle dating back to 1154. A Pierre de Voisins erected the present Chateau on the western outskirts of the Arques in the late 1300's.

The present area of the village of Arques that contains the church is the oldest part and had been organised according to space available with the church forming the southern limit of a rectangular island. An early castle in the west of the village was on the site of the present church bell tower and the evidence is that the village developed as a result of two successive phases of settlement, during the Middle Ages. The east part corresponds to the walled town circa 1291.

Early manuscripts suggest the community goes back to 1011 when Amiel Arques is mentioned as Lord of the place. Numerous conflicts and confrontations have resulted in the changes in the domain of Arques and the inhabitants had to suffer the consequences of the Albigensian Crusade. In 1232 Pierre de Voisins, Simon de Montfort's lieutenant received Arques as part of his new possessions and was granted land upon which to build the present fortified Chateau. Before that time the church of Saint Anne was dedicated to John the Baptist and is constructed in the shape of a Latin cross. It was thought to be 14th century with 19th century restoration work.

Déodat Roche was the village's most notable personage, who during his life had been a magistrate, general Counsellor and Mayor of the locality between 1925 and 1936. He was the founder president of the 'Society for Cathar Souvenirs and Studies' and of the 'Notebook of Cathar Studies'. He was an historian of Catharsis and published several articles on the subject. In 1970 he received the Broquette-Gonin Prize of the French Academy and was passionate about the Life of the Soul in the World beyond. The greater part of his work was written in Arques, which is where he died. His house is on the western edge of the Village Square. …There is an exhibition about Catharism in the Maison de Deodat Roche (in the village of Arques). Open every day in July and August. To determine if Roche knew of any landmarks or signs that point to those treasures would require one to become familiar with Cathar history and to make a detailed examination of Roche's work.

After the fall of Montsegur in 1244, those of the garrison who escaped with their precious items made their way along the old trails towards

Arques where sympathy for the cause still remained. The more valuable items and the bulk of the Cathar treasures were safely hidden, but the inquisitors extracted the secret from those who knew of its whereabouts. In monetary terms the Cathar treasures may not be as valuable as Dagobert's, but its importance should not be underestimated for it is likely to include sacred and priceless books belonging to the Cathar. The Church of the day was interested in suppressing the Cathar heretics and having discovered where these items were hidden were keen to ensure that they were secure forever.

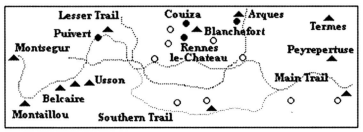

Area around Montsegur circa 1200 AD showing Trails and Chateaus

Figure 19-3

The Cardinals through Poussin made no secret of the *Treasure of Arques* being the principal treasure … 'Et In Arcadia Ego'. What has emerged through this work is the possibility that the Cathar did not place *all their eggs in one basket*. In the *Chatsworth*, besides the shepherds and female there is also *Alpheius the River god* who reappears in the painting, '*Midas washing himself at the source of the Pactolus*'. In effect we could be looking for more than one treasure comprising the *Treasure of Arques*; an entirely new adventure lies with its secrets concealed in more of Poussin's paintings.

CHAPTER 20
THE PAINTINGS.

The times of Nicolas Poussin are referred to earlier and of how the inscription to the painter on his monument at San Lorenzo tells us he speaks *to us in his pictures'*. It is the story of treasure; not just one treasure but more than one. We have already seen that the *Louvre* painting is linked to the Parchments through the symbol and how the letters 'R' and 'C' in the word 'aRCadia' directed us to Rennes-le-Chateau. The shadows in the painting provide clues never before understood and the staffs the shepherds are holding represent the lines of the triangle that is the symbol on Parchment One and which may be drawn through the heads of the shepherd in the painting. However that is not the full story, for the complete message in the word Arcadia directs us from Rennes-le- Chateau to Arques. The *Grave slab* too plays its part in the mystery and its inscription compliments the message deciphered from the *Louvre* and picked up in the earlier *Chatsworth*. It provides the link, the *double indemnity,* from the Standing Stone at Arques with St. Mary Magdalene at Rennes-le-Chateau. The Slab was cleverly designed and is a *Parchment set in Stone.* It was intended to endure and to provide a back up, a link and continuity; even in the event that all else failed, those for whom it was ultimately intended would, in association with Poussin's epitaph, understand its message. We are in no position to know if that is the case and even if there were those who understood they are hardly likely to make it general knowledge.

Unfortunately now, if my story is to be believed the secret is out and all of Poussin's carefully prepared plans are here for all to see.

The *Chatsworth* painting is oil on canvas measuring 101 x 82 centimetres and thought to have been completed around 1627 AD; it is now in the private collection of the Duke of Devonshire at Chatsworth House in England.

The central object in the picture is an ornate sarcophagus with the inscription, 'Et In Arcadia Ego', at which one of the four figures is pointing. A female companion is standing with two shepherds against the tomb, with the River god Alpheius half reclining at their feet and holding a small barrel out of which water is pouring. A sketch of the painting is shown in Figure 20-1. Its potential has not before been explored, nor its hidden secrets considered; it is a very interesting picture. One character in particular, that of *Alpheius, who* is not seen in the *Louvre,* provides a link with other paintings.

Today it is the *Louvre* that is more readily associated with the Treasure of Rennes-le-Chateau; the earlier *Chatsworth* hardly gets a second glance with the lesser pictures, such as the *Midas,* not even being considered. The true importance of the *Chatsworth* did not come to light until the significance of the Standing Stone was understood. It became apparent that just as a line could be drawn through the heads of the shepherds in the *Louvre,* so it was in the *Chatsworth,* with the subsequent results highlighting important discoveries.

Figure 20-1

The story of King Midas is familiar. In Poussin's painting Midas is seen bathing himself from water that is pouring out of a barrel … the same barrel that was shown in the *Chatsworth* and here once again held by *Alpheius the river god.* According to the story the gold that is being washed off Midas finds its way into the river, where it leaves a residue … the river that local tradition equates with the *River of the King's gold* is the River Railsesse near Arques. Accompanying Alpheius in the *Midas* are two cherubs with small barrels out of which water is also pouring and running into the river; each of the cherubs shares the same *hairstyles* as Alpheius. … Alpheius is the name of the river with its tributaries closely associated with Arcadia. It is also noticed that the large forked tree, which was behind the tomb in the *Chatsworth*, is reproduced in the *Midas*.

In the *Louvre* we saw how the symbol on Parchment One could be drawn over the heads of the shepherds in the picture and how breaking down the word 'Arcadia' relayed a message; the *Chatsworth* at first appears less forthcoming, but like the *Louvre* the *Chatsworth* also has its mysteries - whether or not it has its *error* is yet to be discovered. The *Midas* plays a supporting role to the *Chatsworth* and could be a strong indicator of the location of the treasure. However the painting is not the only picture to be of interest in this connection. In his book, 'Poussin's Paintings a Catalogue Raisonne', Christopher Wright reproduces two plates, 105 and 106. The first is entitled, '*Midas at the source of the River Pactolus*', the second, '*Midas washing himself in the Pactolus*'.

At first sight Plate '105' had nothing to commend it and was not further considered, but with hindsight that may require a rethink. The *Chatsworth* predates the *Midas* by two or three years, but the substantive connection between the *Midas* and the *Chatsworth* is confirmed by *Alpheius the river god*. In the *Midas* there is no 'Et In Arcadia Ego', or Tomb. Even so, we see the link with treasure, for King Midas in the story was turned to gold. Such comparisons hardly prove the case that the painting is relevant to the pursuit of the treasure, although it did form part of Cardinal Massimi's collection and Nicolas Poussin painted it.

If the Barberini had commissioned the *Chatsworth* and the *Midas*, there might be other paintings of interest and a search was made to find a companion to the *Louvre*; one that might identify with Rennes-le-Chateau and Rennes les Bains. In the book, 'Nicolas Poussin, Masterpieces 1591 - 1665' there appeared to be a case for consideration. The painting in question is entitled, '*Landscape with three men*", which is an oil on canvas. The painting is 120 x 187 cm. and is in the Museo del Prado, Madrid. In setting out his path to the treasures Poussin had built-in a complex cross-referencing sequence, which we see in the *Louvre, Chatsworth* and the *Midas*.

Three Men

Men with horses

Landscape with Three men

Figure 20-2

The *Landscape* compliments the *Louvre,* although it was first rejected on the grounds that certain aspect of the painting, to which Poussin was quietly drawing attention, was in fact inconsistent with what one could see on the ground. Scenes in the picture are similar to those in a number of Poussin paintings. The range of hills used as the backdrop, the buildings, river and the group of men. What was evident was that the painting, because of the river was not of a scene around Rennes-le-Chateau, nor did it appear to reflect the countryside around Arques.

The presence of the river in the picture might be taken to suggest the river Sals at Rennes les Bains in which case if there was any merit in the picture as far as reference to a treasure was concerned it would have to be that of Dagobert's gold.

In the centre background of the picture is the range of hills that can be compared with those seen in the *Louvre,* but in reverse order (See Plate 10). The map confirms that the hills marked as Cardou, Blanchefort and Rennes-le-Chateau are pictorially in the correct alignment when viewed from Rennes les Bains; it will also be noticed that in the sketch of the painting there is a Mill and a Weir ... albeit they are not now geographically where Poussin shows them. Nonetheless both Mill and Weir are in the immediate vicinity of the church at Rennes les Bains. Towards the centre left of the picture, directly under the distant hill of Rennes-le-Chateau is the projecting eaves of a building that has strong similarities with the Apse of St. Nazaire Et Celse. Further, to the left in the picture, between the branches of the tree is a belfry, not unlike that at St. Mary Magdalene.

The presence of figures in one of Poussin's painting is not unusual, but interest in this particular case is that they are drawn to ones attention, not only by reference in the title to *Three men*, but also by their gestures. Two of the characters were rather notable. The 'shepherd' in the centre of the group of three (facing the viewer) is looking towards the river, whilst the person on his left, with his back to the viewer is pointing towards the buildings. The person on the right of the three is also looking towards the river, his companion towards the Belfry. Slightly closer the river are two other figures standing beside horses; it is possible the wrong conclusions are being drawn from the picture, but the coincidences are striking. Having visited the area and *stood on the very spot* where the painter set up his easel gave one an overwhelming sense of going back in time. Henry Lincoln or anyone who has also stood on the higher ground at Pontils and looked objectively at the site of the old tomb must have experienced similar feelings.

There is something else that is odd about the two figures with the horses. Draped over the back of the nearest horse is the resemblance of a human shape. This would not have attracted attention were it not for the fact in the immediate vicinity of Rennes les Bains is an area known as ... L'Homme Mort - the dead man. (See Fig 8-3)

Perhaps there are too many coincidences and one can easily get carried away, but the more I look at the painting of the *Landscape with three men* the more I am convinced of its purpose.

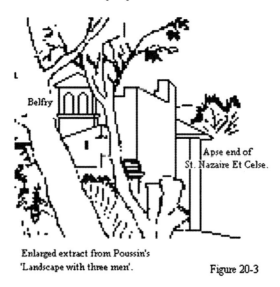

Belfry

Apse end of
St. Nazaire Et Celse.

Enlarged extract from Poussin's
'Landscape with three men'.

Figure 20-3

Poussin was encouraged to use his ingenuity and imagination in his paintings and stonework. He had been told roughly what the Dagobert hoard comprised and that it included the menorah; it is unlikely he saw any of the treasure. The work the painter undertook at St. Mary Magdalene possibly included structural alterations to the Belfry Tower; none of which could have been done without the consent of the Bishop at Carcassonne. It is these works I feel are reflected in the painting.

A complete set of paintings without the knowledge of the *Tomb of Arques* and no idea of the area to which they related would be almost worthless. The Parchments without the *Louvre* painting would also, treasure wise, have little meaning. We now have two independent sets of clues, closely linked, but supporting different treasures.

The Barberini could not foresee the future or that the paintings would pass through the Cardinal's Estate and become spread far and wide, or even destroyed. Poussin took the precaution of setting things in stone as well as in his paintings. However, nothing endures forever and both Cardinal and painter anticipated that knowledge of the secret could pass into obscurity. … *"It is possible that nobody else will ever rediscover (it) in the centuries to come".* Two hundred years after the painter's death someone saw this possibility and determined that the secret should be preserved for posterity.

The *Chatsworth* and the *Midas* were paired in the inventory of Cardinal Camillo Massimi; both being linked to *Alpheius the River God* and the *Treasure of Arques*. The *Louvre* is associated with the *Landscape* and closely linked with the *Treasure of Rennes-le-Chateau*. These four paintings and probably more are part of a set prepared by Poussin for his masters in Rome. Those who knew the secret had no difficulty in seeing the whole picture in the paintings, when they were laid out before them. Others in the centuries to come when the paintings were dispersed, even if they were aware of the secrets, had little to go on and had it not been for the actions of the errant priest Berenger Sauniere knowledge of the treasures would have passed into obscurity.

The Pyrenees, in Poussin's day, was a number of weeks journey away from Rome. When he arrived at his destination he had to accomplish tasks that could have occupied him for quite a while. At the very least he would have been away from home for a number of weeks. At first it was imagined the *Chatsworth* and the *Midas* were studio works, but it is now evident the *Chatsworth* required on-site notes and time arranging with the local mason to build the *Tomb of Arques* and procure and erect the Pierre Dressee or Standing Stone. The *Chatsworth* and the *Midas* were painted around 1627, thirteen years before he left Italy for Paris in 1640: the *Louvre* was completed two years before his journey. It was thought the Parchments, Altar and Grave slab did not appear until 1646, which may still be the case, but the *Chatsworth* and the *Louvre* were sketched before 1627 and realistically all the preparation work, including that planned at Mary Magdalene was close to completion by 1640. This included sketches for the *Landscape* and the *Midas*. It is known that the painter was ill for some time and together with his work on the treasures may account for Poussin stating he was too busy to go to the Court of Louis XIV of France until his work for the Cardinals was finished.

By contrast with the *Tomb of Arques* the *Chatsworth* Tomb is ornate and in a setting that is not unlike that in the *Midas*. The Arques tomb has a weathered top whereas the *Chatsworth* tomb has a flat cover slab; if for no other purpose than to place the skull. Whether it is modelled on an actual tomb somewhere in the area is not possible to say and no attempt has been made to find it. – Indeed, there are no clues to aid ones search. The inscription, 'Et in Arcadia Ego' on the side of the Chatsworth *tomb* in the painting has the word 'Ego' relegated to a lower line; we then read 'Et In Arcadia', leaving us in no doubt that the location is in Arcadia … *and in Arques.*

On the face of it the *Midas* offers little to compare with the *Chatsworth* and the *Louvre*, yet, there is something about it that makes one wonder what deep secret it holds. *King Midas washed himself in the Pactolus* and thereafter that river had a residue of gold. I get the impression we are dealing with more than one Cathar treasure site and perhaps this is the reason for the emphasis on 'Et in Arcadia Ego'. Although it is understood the Cathar did not have great material wealth there were a number of well-to-do families with property and lands amongst the believers. If under the surrender terms some of the Cathar were led to believe that after denouncing their faith they would be allowed to resume normal lives, then their wealth would have been secreted away. It seems evident therefore that we may be looking at more than one treasure site.

In passing it might be worth noting the painting entitled, 'Apollo and Daphne', thought to be in the Alte Pinakothek, Munich, which was abandoned by Poussin and given in its unfinished state to Cardinal Camillo Massimi, is also of interest. The story in Greek Mythology tells of Marsyas challenging Apollo to a musical contest over which King Midas would be the judge. Midas did not find in Apollo's favour, so Apollo punished him by changing the King's ears into the ears of an Ass.

Daphne was the daughter of the River God Alpheius who prayed to the Earth to rescue her from Apollo's pursuits. She was transformed into a Laurel, which Apollo appropriated for poets. To hand there is only an indistinct monochrome copy of the 'Apollo and Daphne' that is rather unhelpful, but in the original picture a golden bowl may be seen, together with Alpheius pouring water from his barrel, as well as a number of cherubs and Daphne. Little more of substance can be offered and it may be the painting has no association with the treasure. Nevertheless one does have suspicions, particularly as it was a later painting by Poussin. The challenge now is to view more of Poussin's paintings to see what other secrets he has hidden with his brushes and paints.

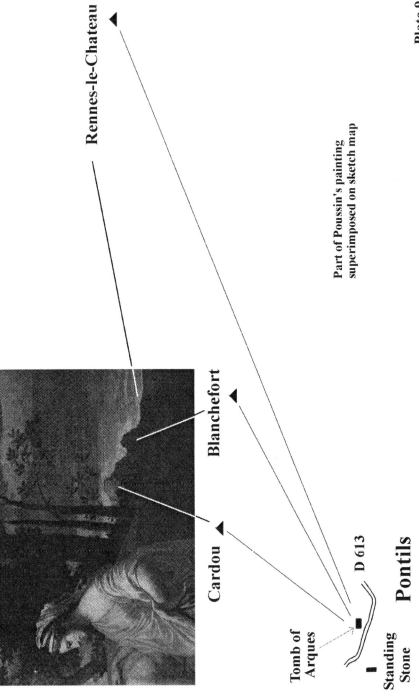

Rennes-le-Chateau

Blanchefort

Cardou

D 613

Tomb of
Arques

Standing
Stone

Pontils

Part of Poussin's painting
superimposed on sketch map

Plate 9

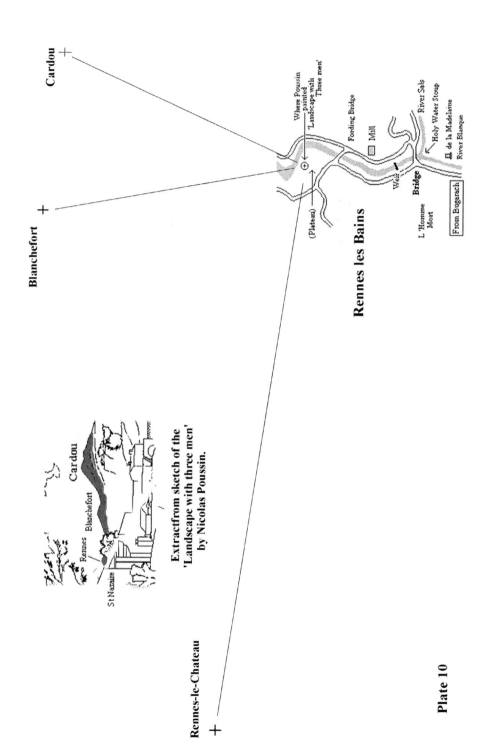

Cardou

Blanchefort

Rennes-le-Chateau

Rennes les Bains

Where Poussin painted 'Landscape with Three men'

(Plateau)

Fording Bridge

Mill

Weir

River Sals

Holy Water Stoup

Il de la Madelaine
River Blanque

L'Homme Mort

Bridge

From Bugarach

Extract from sketch of the 'Landscape with three men' by Nicolas Poussin.

St Nazaire

Rennes

Blanchefort

Cardou

Plate 10

LOST AND FOUND

CHAPTER 21
THE GRAIL AND THE ARK.

Stories of the Grail exploits became popular within Christendom during the late twelfth and early thirteenth-centuries. Although at that time they were still based on the legends of King Arthur and the Knights of the Round Table, greater emphasis was being placed on Biblical events. The Holy Grail as it became known took the form of a dish upon which the food of the Last Supper was served to Jesus and the disciples in the upper room. Of more recent times the Grail is referred to as the Cup from that Last Supper that is said at the Crucifixion to have caught Christ's blood as he hung on the cross.

Chretien de Troyes, who died in 1185, was probable the greatest medieval writer of Arthurian romances and although we know little of his life, we do know that between 1160 and 1172 he lived at Troyes in France. He wrote a number of poems but is chiefly remembered for his unfinished work of Perzival and the story of the Grail.

The origin of the legend of the Grail is thought to the have come from the mystical traditions of the ancient Welsh or Briton cultures. These legends have as their base the earlier Celtic sources from Ireland that tell of a mythical and poetical paradise where maidens at grottoes with wells and springs served travellers from golden bowls and cups. As a result of man's greed the maidens were ravished and the bowls stolen. What had once been a paradise became a barren desert. The legend tells of a heroic quest to discover the place where the natural land meets the lost paradise and to restore the sacred waters. It is a never-ending quest that in the modern idiom we might see it in the song, 'The impossible dream'. Eventually the object of the quest took on the more realistic form of the 'Cup of the Last Supper', The Holy Grail.

Chretien de Troyes' tales began to circulate around the time of the return of the original Knights Templar, from the Holy Land. They brought back with them great treasures, and although their mission had been promoted as a means of protecting pilgrims visiting Jerusalem, they may have let it be known they were also searching for the Holy Grail; romantic notions that were used to conceal the true purpose of the adventure.

The Cup of the Last Supper takes numerous forms. In its grandest and most unlikely form it is a beautiful golden goblet studded with precious stones. It can also be a wooden cup without ornamentation and unattractive. In its simplest form it would have been a rough piece of pottery and subject to a short life. On the night of the Last Supper in that upper room the place settings were very basic. No fine cutlery or matching porcelain, in fact all we are told is that the meal consisted mainly of bread and wine, not much call for a well-set table. The bread Jesus broke to represent His body, and after supper He took the cup ... *do this in remembrance of me*. When the meal was over Jesus and the disciples left the upper room and went their various ways. It is doubtful if anyone would have had the presence of mind to pick up the cup that Jesus used and keep it until the crucifixion. It might also be mentioned that if Jesus were aware someone was taking the cup without the landlord's consent He would not have approved. More to the point, apart from Jesus, no one else would have had knowledge of the events that were shortly to come to pass. Only one of the disciples, the disciple whom Jesus loved, was with Mary the Mother of Jesus at Calvary and scripture makes no mention of the cup or the Grail being present.

In his book entitled 'The Sign and the Seal' Graham Hancock the historical researcher relates an incredible tale and traces the Ark of the Covenant back to Ethiopia. He concludes, and his evidence is quite convincing that the Ark rests in a small chapel in Axum, guarded by one old Priest who never for a moment leaves the building or its compound and denies anyone entry, saying it is too dangerous. Hancock concludes his work by stating that, – *for Ark and Grail is one and the same*.

Two French knights, Hugh des Payens and Godfrey of Saint-Omer, formed the Poor Knights of Christ of the Temple of Solomon, or Knights Templar in Jerusalem in 1119. The order developed from a small military band; its stated aim was to protect pilgrims visiting Palestine after the First Crusade.

The Order obtained papal sanction in 1128 at the ecclesiastical Council of Troyes and was closely patterned on the monastic order of Cistercians. A Grand Master headed the Knights Templar, and under him were three ranks of Knights, chaplains, and sergeants, but only the Knights were allowed to wear the distinctive dress of the order, a white mantle with a large red Latin cross on the back. The headquarters of the Knights Templar remained at Jerusalem until the fall of the city to the Muslims in 1187; the nine original Knights were back in Europe by 1138

Because the Templars regularly transmitted money and supplies between Palestine and Europe, they later developed an efficient banking system, on which the rulers and nobility of Europe came to rely. The knights gradually became bankers for a large part of Europe and amassed great wealth. Their immense riches and power had aroused the envy of secular as well as ecclesiastical powers, and in 1307 the impoverished Philip IV of France, with the aid of Pope Clement V, arranged for the arrest of the French Grand Master Jacques de Molay on trumped-up charges of sacrilege and Satanism. Clement V seized its property and the order was eventually suppressed in 1312.

Chretien de Troyes and later Wolfram von Eshenbach who was also writing stories of the Grail and Parzival at a time around 1160 when the Templars, renowned for their wealth and exploits, as well as continuing the quest for the Holy Grail (Ark of the Covenant) were the subject of romantic legend.

It seems that later Knights of the Order, after the excavations under Temple Mount had failed to uncover the Ark of the Covenant, befriended the exiled Prince Lalibela of Ethiopia. When he returned in triumph to his country in 1185, two years before Jerusalem fell to the Muslims, he had with him a contingent of Templar. The Prince who became King Lalibela would have informed the Knights that what they were looking for in Jerusalem was in fact in his country. If the Knights, as mercenaries, were instrumental in ensuring the King's triumph the least of their reward would have been to see the Ark of the Covenant ... the Holy Grail. Graham Hancock also quotes from B T Evett's translation of Abu Salih's work, *Churches and Monasteries of Egypt and some neighbouring countries*, where he reads:

The Abyssinians possess the Ark of the Covenant, in which are the two tablets of stone inscribed by the finger of God with the commandments which he ordained for the Children of Israel. The Ark of the Covenant is placed upon the altar; it is as high as the knee of a man and is overlaid with gold. Abu Salih was an early 13th century Armenian geographer who would have met with the Templars and it seems was witness to some of the ceremonies surrounding the Ark. It was regularly on displayed and no attempt, as today, was made to conceal it. It also seems that when the Ark was amongst the people neither they nor the priests wore any form of protective clothing, as was the case when the Israelites first possessed it.

The Ark of the Covenant

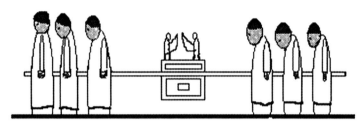

Figure 21-1

The Ark of the Covenant, or of the Testimony was a simple wooden box structure overlain within and without with pure gold. Its dimensions were two and a half cubits (3'9") long, by one and a half cubits (2'3") wide and the same dimension deep. These appear to be the overall dimensions. Assuming the wood to be 2" thick, the internal size, less the thickness of the gold would be 3'5" x 1'11" x 1'11". On this basis I assess the amount of timber to be 3660 cu. inches, or 2 cu. feet. A cubic foot of hardwood weighs 45 lbs, therefore the open box of the Ark weighed about 90 lbs. Pure Cast Gold weighs 1200 lbs. per cubic foot; there being approximately 230 cu. inches (1/16th. of an inch thick) covering the lower part of the box and an inclusive weight of 250 lbs. The weight of the lid or Mercy Seat was at least equal to the 'box'. If the lid or Mercy Seat with the Cherubim were of pure gold the whole unlade Ark, including the rings and carrying staves, would weight about 1000 lbs. ... I am not taking into account the Table mentioned in verse 23, which would have been much the same weight. The Testimony was written on the tablets of stone. There were two pieces. Being practical one has to consider a comfortable weight Moses could carry unaided down a mountain. If the pieces of stone were of such a size to lay flat side by side in the bottom of the 'box' they would be about 20" square by perhaps 1" thick, in all about 50 lbs in weight; not an insignificant addition to the weight of the Ark. The length the Staves or carrying handles had to be of such dimension not to break under the heavy load and be long enough for the priests to comfortably manoeuvre the dangerous 'box'. The number of Priests required to lift the laden Ark will be calculated by dividing its weight by the amount one man might be expected to carry. If one priest could raise just under one hundred weight then twelve men were required, three at each end of each stave.

There is a suggestion the stone tablets contained the power source, but what happened to the first set that Moses threw down upon the ground and smashed. If the power was in the stones and as dangerous as it subsequently proved to be Moses could not have brought it single-handed down from the mountain.

Moses was instructed to present the completed Ark outside the Camp when the Lord would come down and modify the cherubim and place within the box some form of electrical generator. The Lord instructed Moses, '*And thou shalt* (only) *put into the Ark the testimony that I shall give thee*', and that '*nobody will ever lift away the Mercy Seat* (cover) *from the Ark of my Testimony, for in the day that he does he shall surely die*'.

[Leviticus chapter 10. ... sons of Aaron tried to enter the Holy of Holies with burnt offering and were devoured by fire.]. They got too close to the Ark that emitted electrical discharges.

The Mercy Seat had incorporated in it Cherubim or winged angels facing one another from either end. Moses only relates the basic details of the Ark he was instructed to make. (Exodus chapter 25, verse 40 implies the instruction may have taken the form of a sketch). The construction of the wooden box presented no problem, but the Mercy Seat was a different matter. The distance between the faces of the cherubim's and the shape and position of their wings needed to be more precise than just leaving it to Moses. It was where Moses and the Lord could talk with one another: a method of communication, which today any youngster let, alone a communications expert would soon identify. The receiver and transmitter were housed in the *heads* of the cherubim. However all transmitters and receivers are of little use unless connected to a power source; and in the days of Moses that source of power was in the Ark.

This twenty first century world of ours boasts numerous forms of electricity generators, but few which are portable and even less, which require no servicing, fueling or recharging. Two sources come to mind. The one is Solar Energy the other is radioactive. For the purposes of powering a radio, a solar power panel would have been adequate. Its drawback would be twofold. First it would need to be a separate unit making it vulnerable to damage. Secondly, it is hardly a set-up to inspire a sense of mystery and awesome power with which the Lord could demonstrate His omnipotence. In short, one deliberate blow, a mechanical fault or a silly accident would bring contempt and derision upon Moses and his Lord, so I am left with the other form of power to consider, namely radioactive.

169

Before examining this other source there is an essential component associated with the type of communication system that I am suggesting was employed in connection with the Ark. It is commonplace these days to see individuals like doctors, part time firemen, service engineers and the like carrying 'Pagers'. It is a simple device that picks up a signal from a base unit indicating a person's attention is required. Something like a pager would have been needed for the Lord to tell Moses to, 'come to the telephone', and visa versa. This instrument would either have been in Moses' possession or with someone like the High Priest or his aide, who were always within the bounds of the Tabernacle or Temple. In the Bible there is reference to something called the, 'Urim and Thummim', which was a part of the High Priests Costume.

These references are in, Leviticus chapter 8 verse, 8; Numbers chapter 27, verse 21; Deuteronomy chapter 33, verse 8; 1st Book of Samuel, chapter 28, verse 6 and Ezra chapter 2, verse 63. - The verse in 1st Book of Samuel, chapter 28, verse 6, is particularly interesting, *'And when Saul enquired of the Lord, the Lord answered him not, neither by dreams, nor URIM, nor by prophets'*. The Urim and Thummin is clearly associated with making contact with the Lord, and in my opinion, was a PAGER. There is no explanation for the Lord not answering Saul. I will however add that the 'Pager' by that date had been around for 430 years.

Also in the 1st Book of Samuel, chapter 4 we read the following, a warning from the Lord that he would *destroy the house of Eli.* The Israelites were once more engaged in battle with the Philistines, but something went drastically wrong and the Philistines capture the Ark. ... in chapter 5.1, the Philistines hold the Ark ... The source of power was still in the Ark at that time. … In verses 3, 4, and in verses 7 and 8 the Philistines are smitten with haemorrhoids. They discuss sending the Ark back to the Israelites, verse 9. More Philistines are smitten in their secret parts with haemorrhoids. They had done what Moses was expressly forbidden to do – they had *opened the box.* – More than that, they took out the power source and did not put it back. In chapter 6, verse 1. - *'And the Ark of the Lord was in the country of the Philistines seven months'*. ... Verse 19, *'And He smote the men of Bethshemesh* (House of the Sun) *because they had, looked into the Ark of the Lord, even he smote of the people fifty thousand and three score and ten (50,070): and the people lamented because the Lord had smitten many of the people with a great slaughter'*. – The Philistine's curiosity got the better of them and they died in the thousands. The cause of their death was undoubtedly exposure to extremely large doses of radiation. Panic seized them, nobody now wanted the Ark anywhere near them. *'Take it back, take it back'*. The Lord God of the Israelites was dreadful in His dealing with

The Secret Church

them. Not only did the Philistines take the Ark back, they bestowed gifts on the Children of Israel in an attempt to appease the wrath of their God. The power unit in the Ark was probably tipped out onto the ground and became a source of fatal attraction. The horrible consequences of the Philistines actions terrified them and no one would go near it to return the object to its box. The likelihood is that the dangerous object was pushed into a pit or prepared hole in the ground where it was covered. The site of ancient *Bethshemesh* is today approximately 15 kilometres west of Jerusalem. The half-life of uranium that was possibly the core of a mini reactor (generator) once in the Ark of the Covenant is 24,000 years.

It would be a simple (time consuming) but interesting exercise for some one with a Geiger counter to wander around the area of ancient Bethshemesh to check if the power source that was once in the Ark of the Covenant still exists.

The Bible Concordance defines haemorrhoids as, *tumours and piles.* The medical dictionary says haemorrhoids are enlarged varicose veins in the lower part of the rectum, and can be symptomatic of Radiation Sickness, which is, a disease caused by excessive exposure to a radioactive source; principally the intestine and marrow are affected. The severity of the illness is proportional to the degree of exposure. In the case of the Philistines it appears the dose was short, massive and lethal, leading them to conclude, *'No one is safe in the presence of the Lord, this holy God'.*

There was nothing 'mystical' about whatever was in that 'box'. Its terrible power was real; it was radioactive and could only be approached by a priest wearing covering akin to today's *standard radiation protective clothing.*

The priests who attended the Ark were given detailed instructions for the type of clothes, which had to be worn; washing before and after was essential. - Leviticus chapter 16, verse 23. ... Aaron the High Priest, after making sacrifice for atonement for the sins of the people in the Holy of Holies, where the Ark was kept, when he came out into the Tabernacle had to remove his *Protective* clothes and leave them before washing and dressing to go out to meet the people. The remains of the sacrificial bullock and one goat, which had been taken into the Holy of Holies, was removed and burnt. The other goat, the Scapegoat, upon which the sins of the people were lain, after the High Priest had laid hands on it was led away into the wilderness by a 'fit' or healthy man. That man could not come back into the camp until he had washed himself and his clothes. Ritual, just ritual one might say, but ritual can sometimes be borne out of necessity; I suggest there was a very good reason why things were done the way

171

they were and in this case it was because of the actual threat of Radiation Contamination.

In these enlightened times with nuclear power having being around for sixty years and commonplace in the lives of today's generation, the proposal that in Moses' day (1490 BC) there is remarkable evidence for a form of energy that has similar characteristics, may not sound so absurd.

The Lord must have had His reasons for providing such a powerful means of generating the electrical current, which possessed the potential to *light a city*, in order to operate the communication system. It was more than adequate for the job and exceedingly dangerous to give to Moses and his priests, without proper safeguards. It never the less, by its awesome power gave Himself and Moses a strong psychological advantage over the rebellious Children of Israel and terrified the enemy.

The Urim and Thummin (Pager) may have been little more than a simple buzzer to attract attention. It was a two-way device that enabled Moses or the High Priest also to contact the Lord. It had its own power source and its appearance remarkably resembled a basic telephone keypad with its twelve (buttons) precious stones.

Referring again to verse in the 1st. Book of Samuel chapter 28 verse 6. *… Saul enquired of the Lord, and the Lord answered him not neither by dreams, nor Urim, nor by Prophets'*. That was in 1058 BC. … 107 years earlier in I Samuel chapter 3., the Lord called Samuel by name a number of times. Old Eli the High Priest instructed the young lad to answer the Lord direct. Verse 7, states, *'Samuel did not yet know the Lord, neither was the word of the Lord yet revealed unto him'*. The interesting thing about the Lord calling to Samuel was that it appeared to be other than by using the Urim and Thummin. The Lord did not use the Pager, had He done so Eli would have known; certainly young Samuel would have been aware of the purpose of a functioning Pager. The Lord, by some means was calling Samuel direct from the cherubim's above the Mercy Seat. The Pager was probably not working and had been out of service a long time before Saul had tried 'ringing the Lord' in 1058 BC.

The Lord's voice was very faint and only audible to young Samuel's ears. At that time the power source was still in the Ark, and the means of communicating with the Lord was clearly possible. Everything was fully functional except it seems the Pager or Urim and Thummin, which was either out of order or had been in some way 'switched off'.

The Ark of the Covenant was in the Tabernacle at Shiloh with Eli and from there, possibly for the last time, was taken out to help the Israelites in their battle with the Philistines. When a messenger came to Eli and told of the loss of the Ark and of the death of the High Priest's two sons (as related by Samuel) the old man appears to have suffered a heart attack on hearing the new and died at 89 years of age. The fact that the Philistines had been able to take the Ark is also very interesting and I believe, not disassociated with a non-functioning Pager. On past occasions whenever the Israelites had gone out to battle, carrying the Ark before them, the *Lord was with them* – He was directing the battle - and they had prevailed in the fight.

Solomon's Temple or the House of Yahweh was specifically designed and built to house the Ark of the Covenant. It was made off-site (prefabricated) so that when the building was finally being erected it was assembled so that … '*there was neither hammer nor axe nor any tool of iron heard in the House whilst it was in building*'.

It is calculated that the length of the carrying staves for the Ark was slightly less than thirty feet. The House of Yahweh had internal measurements of 30 feet by 90 feet and was divided into two parts. The Holy of Holies being 30 feet square on plan and was closed off by folding wooden doors. The Staves length was determined on an assessment of the weights involved and a safe distance from the box by a protected priest.

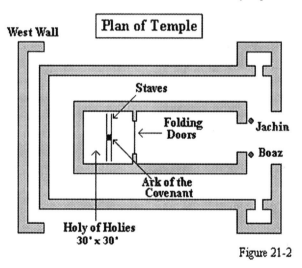

Figure 21-2

The Holy of Holies in Solomon's Temple allowed barely enough room to manoeuvre the Ark within its sanctuary, where it was to be permanently left with the carrying Staves in place. ... (Exodus, chapter 25, verse 15). … ' *The Staves shall be put in the rings of the Ark; they shall not be taken from it* '. Indeed, given the confines of the Arks resting place the Staves could not be easily removed, if as I imagine, it was placed, as my sketch of the Temple suggests, so that the High Priest correctly approached it on the Day of Atonement ...where the Lord said, *'I will meet with thee and commune with thee'*. (Verse 22).

However, when the Ark of the Covenant was installed in the House of the Lord not only did the priests, *'Drew out the staves, that the ends of the staves were seen out in the Holy Place, before the oracle, and they were not seen without: and there they are unto this day'*. (1st Book of Kings, chapter 8, verse 8). In other words they disobeyed the Lord's command. ... Further (verse 9), they looked inside the Ark. ... *'There was nothing in the Ark save the two tablets of stone, which Moses put there at Horeb'*.

The Ark had lost its power and could be handled with ease, without the staves or fear of instantaneous death, by priests requiring no protective garments.

One hundred and forty years had passed since the Philistines had taken away the Ark's power until it finally rested in the House of the Lord. A further three centuries later, in 710BC – according to Graham Hancock – during the reign of Manasseh, the evil King of Judah, the Ark of the Covenant was removed from the Temple to begin its extended journey to Axum in Ethiopia. In its sanctuary, where no one is permitted to see it, a solitary priest who wears no protective clothing guards it day and night. What remains a mystery is the whereabouts of the cherubim (the communicator), the fire (generator) and the Urim and Thummin (Pager).

In the Book of Amos, chapter 9, verse 11, we read, ... 'In that day I will raise up the Tabernacle of David which is fallen, and close up the breaches thereof; and I will raise up his ruins, and I will build it as in the days of old'. – If the prophesy is fulfilled not only will the Temple at Jerusalem be rebuilt the Ark will be restored to its rightful place and all will see the Holy Gail ... the Ark of the Covenant.

Sauniere's Altar

Station 1

Station XIV

Plate 11

Fireplace

Sacristy

Approach to
St Nazaire Et Celse

Skeleton and King

Knight's Tombstone

Plate 12

CHAPTER 22
THE KNIGHTS TEMPLAR
AND ROSSLYN CHAPEL.

Solomon was the son and successor of King David his father and regarded as the greatest king of Israel. He will be principally remembered for his legendary wisdom and the building of the Temple at Jerusalem. His wisdom was tested when two harlots each confronted him claiming to be mother of the same baby. He drew a sword to cut the baby in half, whereupon the real mother pleaded with him for mercy and that the baby should be spared and given to the other woman. Her case was proven. Solomon became famous as a sage and poet as well as being renowned for his wealth. The writer Rider Haggard romanticised this illustrious King in his book and subsequent film, King Solomon's Mines.

David who had been given the plan of the Temple in writing by the hand of the Lord presented it to Solomon. All the refined gold and silver for the vessels for the Temple was provided by David and gold for the pattern of the chariot of the cherubim's, that spread out their wings, and covered the Ark of the Covenant of the Lord. The Temple at Jerusalem was to be a permanent House for the Lord and the Holy of Holies would be where the Ark of the Covenant rested.

In 1065 BC the first Temple was dedicated; Pharaoh Shishak plundered it in 956 BC. Joash restored the Temple in 878 BC and Hezekiah in 726

BC cleansed it. During the evil reign of Manasseh in 697 BC he polluted the Temple, which was repaired by Josiah in 677 BC. In 588 BC it was spoiled by the Chaldeans then rebuilt by Zerubbabel in 535 BC following the decree of Cyrus of Persia. It was finished and dedicated in 515 BC.

The last Temple, which was constructed by Herod, was said to have been magnificent although few details exist. Its destruction came about with the fall of Jerusalem after the Jewish rebellion in AD 67 when the Roman Legions under Titus overran the City. A number of precious artefacts such as the Menorah were looted and taken along with Jewish captives to Rome. This is commemorated on the Arch of Titus, which was built in AD 81, eleven years after the event and stands next to the entrance to the Forum in Rome depicting his triumph at Jerusalem. A year or eighteen months before the city of Jerusalem fell to Titus the task of concealing the Temple treasures had begun and was substantially complete before the City was taken. Although the Romans seized an amount of spoil including the menorah and personal wealth, much was undiscovered and left in the ruins.

Centuries later knowledge or rumours of there being a huge treasure hidden at Jerusalem began to circulate and in the late 10th and early 11th centuries stories that there was treasure under Temple Mount were being taken seriously. The spoils taken by Titus consisted of little more than a few items from the Temple and certainly did not include the Ark of the Covenant.

The Knights would not have gone to the Holy Land on a vague pretext. They must have received persuasive information, either by word of mouth or from a very reliable source, such as a document leading them to conclude their 'crusade' would not be a waste of time and energy. They knew roughly where to search and spent a number of years excavating under the Temple Mount. It follows that if it took them so long to find the treasure the chances are it had been well concealed over a period of time, some of the hiding places dating back for centuries.

The evidence suggests that the Knights Templar circa 1130 AD found a great deal of treasure, but which did not include the Ark of the Covenant ... the Holy Grail! Originally it was thought the Templars found an inventory of the treasure and knew precisely where it all was. This now seems unlikely given the time it took them to uncover the hoards. The Knights Hugh des Payens and Godfrey of St. Omer who knew the extent of the Dagobert hoard would be aware of the possibilities that much of the Temple treasure did not fall into the hands of Titus and consequently was not recovered by the Visigoths when Rome itself was sacked. There would be every chance the Knights had visited the church at Rennes les Bains and knew exactly the extent of Dagobert's hoard. It is probable that some of the treasure was used to finance the Knights trip to the Holy Land.

The Copper Scroll inventory found in Cave 111 of the Dead Sea Scrolls was at first considered to refer to the treasure under Temple Mount, but it proved not to be the case. The quantities of treasure linked with the scroll does not equate with the huge amounts found by the Knights. Had the Templars possessed such a comprehensive document, locating the treasure would have made their task considerably easier. There was no document and the Knights spent eight or nine years excavating under the Temple Mount.

Jerusalem had been overrun numerous times prior to 70AD and it is possible previous generations of Temple Priests had stored valuables beneath the Temple on those occasions. In fact, it was probably standard practice whenever trouble loomed to store the most valuable Temple artefacts in a safe place and the access sealed. Pharaoh Shishak is recorded as plundering Jerusalem in 956 BC, but he did not remove all the Temple treasure, nor did he take away the Ark of the Covenant. Knowledge of much that was secreted away and its exact place of concealment might have been lost. Almost 80 years elapsed before Joash restored the Temple in 878 BC, two generations of people. Similar occurrences took place at three or four periods in history over a span of one thousand years. If it was the practice for the priests to conceal the Temple valuables at the first sign of trouble it is entirely possible that even if a complete inventory was kept at that time such an inventory could easily be lost. The Knights Templar located huge amounts of gold, silver and other precious objects found in numerous separate caches hidden beneath the Temple Mount. Scrolls and talents of gold, vessels, gold, silver, sprinkling basins, cups, sacrificial bowls and vessels. There were garments and other artefacts beyond price, candlesticks, lamps and tongs of gold. Bowls, snuffers, basins, spoons, censers and untold numbers of gold and silver vessels. All similar if not some of the original items once in Solomon's Temple and replicated in the Second Temple built by Herod; these were amongst the treasure uncovered by the Templars, but no Ark of the Covenant, it had been lost to the Jews centuries before the Knights arrived in Jerusalem. This rules out a suggestion that the Ark or any part of it is associated with Dagobert's gold, or the so-called Treasure of Rennes-le-Chateau.

In going to Jerusalem the Knights were, if they were searching for treasure, either on a fool's errand or acting on reliable information. What they unearthed amounted to much more than is set out on the Copper Scroll. A rough assessment of the total weight of gold might be based on the three walls of the Holy of Holies being covered in gold. If the gold were only 1.5 millimetres thick there would be almost 5600 kilograms or 12,750 lbs of the precious metal lining the walls. At current prices it runs into many billions of pound sterling. However, there are those who consider that the Temple of Solomon was adorned with over 500 tons of gold and silver. If some of this was also below Temple Mount, or if a similar amount of silver and gold was used in Herod's Temple then the Knights of the Temple of Solomon were very busy indeed. The Templars are rumoured to have shipped the precious cargoes across the Mediterranean to southern France and then to a place of concealment; where it has remained to this day.

The stated purpose of the Templars being formed in Jerusalem was in order to protect pilgrims in the Holy Land, in reality they were using it as a smoke screen to cover the quest for the Holy Grail. Either way it was looked upon as a noble cause.

The Knights Templar was a medieval religious and military order established at the time of the Crusades. It was Baldwin II, king of Jerusalem who gave them quarters in a wing of the royal palace in the area of the former Jewish Temple; from this they derived their name. The Templars wealth and power became too much for the impoverished Philip IV of France and with the aid of Pope Clement V in 1307 he saw his chance to improve his finances and effectively put an end to the Templars. In England King Edward II also sought to disband the order.

The Templar knew the whereabouts of Dagobert's gold and after returning from the Holy Land with the treasures also used the church at Rennes les Bains as a place of concealment for some of the more priceless artefacts recovered by the Knights from under Temple Mount. The Templar wealth together with their moral code and chivalry had encouraged large numbers of followers to join them, thus adding to their lands, communal wealth and power. Over a period of one hundred and fifty years the Order became very prosperous, to the envy of Church and State alike. Shortly before 1307 some of the Templar, sensing there was a growing plot against them made plans to safe guard all they could. Large amounts of valuables were secretly put aboard ships bound for chosen to destinations. Some of the wealth went to England with the bulk of it being taken to Scotland. Over the centuries much of the treasure had been committed to military campaigns benevolent works and in support of the Order. Sir William St Claire spent huge sums of money, possibly equivalent to more than £25 million pounds Stirling over forty years in the building of Rosslyn Chapel. If any of the original treasure the first migrant Templars brought with them still remains it could be in the vaults at Rosslyn Chapel.

In their book, 'The Second Messiah', Messrs Knight and Lomas, quote a deciphered translation by Ward, of something called the, 'Transmission of Larmenius', which in essence contained a curse. It stated, 'that they, the Scot Templars, deserters of the Order ... be outside the circle of the Temple ... blasted by an anathema'. We might ask why such a curse was directed at those Knights who escaped the persecutions and fled to Scotland. The reason it seems is that not only had the departing Templar taken with them as much wealth as they could carry, they also took knowledge of the Great Secret of the Knights Templar. The Templar left in France who managed to evade the terror of 1307 not only lost their own possessions, but as an Order they also lost knowledge of the Great Secret.

Many years later, perhaps for similar reasons as those considered by the Barberini family, someone with knowledge of the Templar Secret engaged a highly trusted and respected member of the Order to set in stone the Secret that is beyond price. Today anyone without the *key* and special knowledge of Templar ritual would understand Sir William St Clair's 'coding' at Rosslyn, or become aware of the treasure's existence; even if they did they may never determine where the treasure lies. Just as Poussin related in his paintings the secret of the Treasure of Arques and Dagobert's gold and similarly as Sauniere left us his icons and pictures. Centuries earlier Sir William had left his guide to the treasure in Rosslyn Chapel, which is described as a place full of mystery. Knight and Lomas in their book, 'The Hiram Key' suggest that after Sir William had completed his design for the Chapel he introduce ritual to aid future generations of Templar to discover the *Key*. The words in the ritual state that - *Nothing is wanting but the Key.* And - *If thou canst comprehend these things, thou knowest enough.* The words were intended for those in the Order, no one else. Nicolas Poussin said - *It is possible that nobody else will ever rediscover in the centuries to come.* No one other than those *of the priesthood* (Cardinals) - *He* reckoned without the minor priest Berenger Sauniere. The weakest link of any secret is a chance discovery.

Rosslyn Chapel was founded and constructed by Sir William St. Clair the third and last St. Clair Prince of Orkney in 1446. The present Chapel is only part of what was intended and took about forty years in the building. Sir William died in 1484 at the age of ninety years and is buried in the Chapel. Rosslyn is well worth a visit and to acquire a copy of the short history of Rosslyn by the Earl of Rosslyn. Since the publishing of the book, The Da Vinci Code by Dan Brown the Chapel has seen a marked increase in the number of visitors. Those who now crowd the little Chapel can only stand and stare and like Dan Brown leave none the wiser, unaware of the real secrets that Sir William St Claire has set in stone.

At the present time, in order to arrest the deteriorating structure of the Chapel it is protected with a purpose made canopy, which although hiding the structure from traditional views nevertheless affords a rare opportunity to safely scale the heights and look down on the building from above.

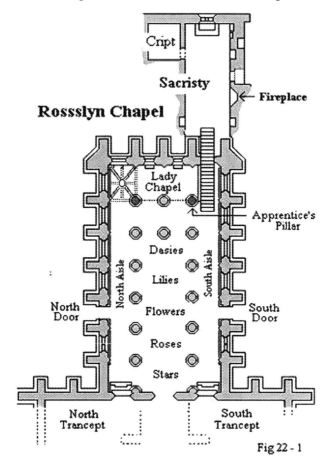

Fig 22 - 1

The building is a masterpiece of intricate carvings amongst which are two beautifully carved pillars, one known as the Mason's pillar, the other as the Apprentice's pillar. The Chapel is also famous for its myriad of heads of Green men. Sir William's true intent in creating Rosslyn Chapel, which today is mainly seen as a unique place of worship is now lost on even those of the Order of Knights Templar. Today it is seen as a House of God, but was once described as a, 'House of idolatry and not a place appointed for teaching the Word and for ministering the sacraments'. St. Mary Magdalene at Rennes-le-Chateau and Rosslyn Chapel has much in common. As places of worship the proper use has become secondary; in each we now look to solve a mystery.

All the indications are that beneath Rosslyn Chapel there are vaults. A John Slezer, writing in 1693, knew of bodies of the barons of Rosslyn found well preserved after four score years in the vaults. The access point has long disappeared though we might assume that Sir William St. Clair did not have to lift slabs or dig in the chapel floor to uncover steps each time he required to go down into the vaults; there was an easier way. Numerous attempts have been made within the chapel proper to locate access to the vaults. Indeed, for security purposes it would have been foolish to make it so.

Many of the carvings in the chapel tell their own story. For instance the heads of the Apprentice, the mason and the Apprentice's mother; the Sinclair engrailed Cross; angels playing musical instruments; Lucifer the fallen angel, shown upside-down and bound in ropes that end in a 'Z'. When the carving is inverted the ends of the ropes still read 'Z' and Lucifer is then looking up – to the ceiling. There is the interesting carving of corn grown by American Indians – Columbus did not discover America until fifty years after Rosslyn was constructed.

Figure 22-2

Other unusual carvings are to be noted such as the vaulted ceiling over the Choir, also the seven deadly sins and the seven virtues where a stone in the lintel is misplaced; 'Charity' and 'Anger' are each in the wrong sequence. Sir William was meticulous in all aspects of the design and building of Rosslyn and such a careless mistake seems unlikely, particularly when it could easily have been corrected. If deliberate, its' meaning at the moment appears obscure.

In the Northeast corner of the Lady Chapel, on the vaulting rib that runs northeast to southwest there are figures with skeletons. These carvings known as the *danse macabre* or dance of death are shown in the Rosslyn Guidebook with an enlarged photographic section. In the top carving we see the skeleton standing to the right of the King and touching the king's elbow. The king's forearm and finger appear to be pointing up to his rod of office in his left hand. However, the king's finger is actually touching his chest. The *danse macabre* they may be, but they also appear to offer another interpretation that tells a different story altogether. Most of the characters on both the vaulted ribs are not easily read; even so it is clear on closer examination the description in the Guidebook is incorrect.

Rosslyn Chapel was built to house a secret meant only for Grand Masters of the order of Templar who could read the signs; it was not intended for the rank and file or the public at large. The paradox Sir William faced was that in openly displaying clues to a secret he risked allowing it to fall into the wrong hands, if only by chance. Once it is understood there is a *key* people will look for it and a renewed quest for a 'Holy Grail' will catch the public imagination; more than ever we are witnessing such an interest at Rosslyn. Should that key ever be located and understood it will allow in part the unlocking of the true secrets of Rosslyn Chapel.

Head of Green Man

Figure 22-3

Rosslyn Chapel, inside and out is full of the carvings of heads of green men; there are over one hundred such carvings, yet only the heads. ... King Dagobert 11 was killed and beheaded in the Forest of Woevres in 691AD.

Later the remains of the king's headless body were taken to lie with his treasure. The skull in the Templar insignia represents the missing head of Dagobert and the crossbones are the lines through the hills that are found in the symbol on Parchment One and which were recognised by Sauniere.

One of the charges laid against the Templar by their inquisitors in 1307 was that they worshipped a head, believed by some to be the head of John the Baptist or even that of Jesus. The Knights did not deny using the head or skull as part of their ritual and insignia although they would have denied the trumped up charges made against them. Those who knew the secret of the skull, probably under extremes of torture, disclosed it that it represented the place of Dagobert's treasure where the Templar gold could be found. There is no indication in anything Poussin portrayed three hundred and fifty years later that the Barberini cardinals knew of other Templar sites; the Templar simply hijacked both the symbol and the location for their own purposes.

The Knights Templar secret was handed down through the St. Clair's and known in its entirety by the builder of Rosslyn. Early in the twelfth century it was the original Knights who excavated below the Temple Mount in Jerusalem where they discovered treasures and knowledge of their find quickly spread and earned then further fame and fortune. The building of Rosslyn Chapel consumed a great deal of time and money; indeed it was extravagant in the use of both. Poussin achieved far more with far less resources, he spread his clues, and they were not all in one place. Like Sir William Sauniere concentrated all the information one requires finding the treasure in one building. At Rosslyn it was where the Templars met and reminders to aid their ceremonies and rituals were all around them. In Sauniere's case there was no secret society, no group or noble cause to whom his clues were directed.

Sir William would not have committed his money and mason's time in carving so many Green men had there been no good reason for doing so. The figure above one hundred that makes sense is arrived at by multiplying 9 by 12 and whilst an explanation is offered for the '9', there is as yet no firm idea what may constitute the '12'. There are, apart from the Mason and Apprentice's pillars twelve structural pillars, but there are other carvings that could number around 12 in total. The Green men are as numerous as the 'trees of the forest' ... the Forest of Woevres. The most prominent head is covered with and surrounded by eight stems of leaves, a pattern which is picked up again in arches of the Lady Chapel where we find eight ribs radiating from above its' pendant boss. The suspended Pendant represents the Head or Skull. Poussin uses it on the *Chatsworth* Tomb, Sauniere shows it in his Station of the Cross, it is part of the Templar

185

insignia - it is Dagobert's head and it points to Rennes les Bains ... And it means treasure.

Stanley James in his reading of the priest Berenger Sauniere seems to think that the 'cave' where the treasure lies has associations attributed to the Templar. The 'door' to the 'cave' is in the form of a skull as Sauniere also shows on the frontispiece picture to the Altar in St. Mary Magdalene. Above the gateway to the Cemetery of that Church we find the Skull and Crossbones, and interestingly that insignia is in the picture of Station 'X11' of the cross in Rennes les Bains church. If the Abbe Boudet did locate the treasure and descended into the cave and was responsible for that particular Station of the Cross-in his church, this would be further confirmation of Templar interest in St Nazaire Et Celse.

Figure 22-4

To the left of the South doorway in Rosslyn Chapel is the carving of a Knight on horseback with his Sergeant at arms, similar to the *Knight's Tombstone* in the church of St. Mary Magdalene in Rennes-le-Chateau and the lifelike statue on the column outside the Temple Church in London. Sir William would not have known of the Knight's Tombstone in St Mary Magdalene but he was familiar with what it represented.

The Knight on horseback is one of a number of plinths, which at one time supported small carved figures. The plinth carvings tell a story of their own that has yet to be understood. The small statues, which played a part in that story have long since disappeared, the likelihood is that shortly before the chapel fell in to disuse around 1592 they taken down into the vaults where they remain to this day.

The Chapel is full of mysterious carvings that in a number of instances are shown to hold obscure secondary meanings. Take for example the flower section of the Chapel ceiling; it might read something like this … *Man is as grass the flower of the field, which today is and tomorrow is cast into the oven.* One does not have to be overly clever to understand what Sir William is telling us. … Oven is fire, Fire is fireplace and Fireplace is Sacristy.

The Sacristy is by far the oldest part of the Chapel and as no way is found down into the vaults from within the main building the obvious place to look for the access would be in the Sacristy. If what John Slezer wrote in 1693 were true, then he was given access to the underground chambers and visited the vaults.

William St. Clair began to build Rosslyn Chapel in 1446 in the reigns of James 1 and James 1V at a time when civil war erupted in Scotland. It was also a time when, as is mentioned in the Rosslyn Guide, according to Father Richard Augustine Hay, 'Prince William (William St. Clair), his age creeping on him, came to consider how to spend his remaining days and to build a house for God's service, of most curious work'. … Most curious work indeed! Atop one of the pillars is a damaged carving showing an angel rolling away the stone from Christ's tomb. Interestingly, the angel behind the right hand edge of the stone is larger than the other angel. Moreover, it is the larger angel's right hand that is holding the stone. This picture may be a pointer to the access for the vault and to put it into context is seen here as a clue understood to mean that the right hand reveal of the fireplace in the Sacristy is the point of access to the vaults. It is believed that originally the right hand reveal of the hearth was in the form of a 'rolling' or sliding stone and therefore the 'doorway to the vaults' below Rosslyn Chapel. If indeed that access were via the Sacristy fireplace the right hand side would be favourite. A simple and non-intrusive test would be to drill with a masonry bit low down through the wall to the right of the fireplace. If this were to locate a void a miniature camera probe could be inserted to show the flight of steps going down from the hearth.

Sir Walter Scott asserts in his epic poem, the 'Lay of the last Minstrel', that when *fate was nigh*, when trouble came to Rosslyn, access to the vaults was concealed behind a roaring fire in the Sacristy. It would not have been difficult for a sliding stone slab to be fitted as a reveal to the hearth and used as the access point. The outer wall thickness is lost in the bedrock immediately outside the Sacristy, which could easily conceal a recess for the stone.

During the Civil War in 1650 Oliver Cromwell's troops stabled horses in the Chapel. Had access to the vaults been from the Chapel floor it would have been discovered. Forty years later when John Slezer visited the vaults he reported that Princes of Orkney and Barons were buried in the building. The indication is that their remains were interred from within the in the Sacristy. Sir Walter Scott in 1805 was more specific, stating that there were twenty uncoffin'd Barons in the Vaults.

The Chapel was abandoned for almost one hundred and fifty years until in 1736 a James St Clair glazed the windows for the first time, repaired the roof and laid flagstones on the floor. Interestingly no direct link from the Chapel proper to the vaults was discovered at that time. It may also be assumed that was when the stonework around the fireplace in the Sacristy was altered to seal the access to the vaults.

The most admired and beautiful of all the carvings at Rosslyn is the Apprentice's pillar at the top of which, overlooking the stairs to the Sacristy, is a representation of Isaac lying bound upon the altar. Adjacent is a ram caught in a thicket. At the base of the pillar are eight dragons and from their mouths comes the vine that winds itself upward around the pillar. The dragons are thought to be dragons from Scandinavian mythology said to lie at the base of a great Ash tree that bound together heaven, earth and hell. Abraham's fire is taken as a reference to the fire in the sacristy with the spiral vines on the pillar representing the spiral steps going down into the vaults below the Chapel.

The other ornate pillar is the Mason's pillar and together may be seen as the two pillars of Solomon's Temple, Boaz and Jachin; Boaz being the great-grandfather of David King of Israel and Jachin who was the High Priest. The significance of this was not lost on Knight and Lomas who in their book, The Hiram Key demonstrated the geometry of Rosslyn in association with Solomon's Temple. The history of Rosslyn Chapel is linked with the St Clair's and is well represented in the guide to Rosslyn Chapel by the Earl of Rosslyn. The Rosslyn Chapel Trust, a registered charity, was set up in 1996.

Sir William St. Clair was burdened with a secret that weighed heavily upon him and like the subsequent Cardinals of Rome and to a lesser extent the priest Berenger Sauniere he needed to, *loosen the ties that bound him.* He was custodian of a fabulous secret far greater than that implied in the words of the Abbe Fouquet, quoting Poussin, that, *Nothing now on this Earth can prove of better value nor be its equal.* Sir William's Chapel was 40 years in the building with much of that time taken up with design and detail that provided an overall picture so complex, yet so simple that, *nothing is wanting but the key.*

Poussin laid down a secret that was discovered in part by the priest of Rennes who in turn appeared obligated to tell the world he had found gold and leave us a legacy until now unresolved. The painter used his artistic ability and creative genius to hand down cleverly crafted and timeless pictures such as Les Berger's d'Arcadie. Sauniere left us his plaster and paint statues and icons to give us the story of the Treasure of Rennes-le-Chateau. Sir William had much earlier used stone and intricate carvings at Rosslyn. The painter's work has been seen only for its artistic beauty. The priest's handiwork at St. Mary Magdalene is considered by the Church Authorities to be no more than the basis of curiosity and tall story telling. The intricate and mysterious stonework in Rosslyn Chapel is nowadays looked upon as enrichment in a 'House of God'.

It has been demonstrated that particular paintings by Nicolas Poussin are more than just works of art resulting in mysteries of St. Mary Magdalene being unravelled. … Let us now look at aspects of Rosslyn Chapel in a little more detail.

Sir William's overall plan was on a grander scale than for the Chapel we see today. The Rosslyn Guide states that Rosslyn Chapel, or the collegiate Chapel of St Matthew, was in fact only part of what was intended. A large cruciform building with a tower at its centre was proposed. The foundations of the Nave were excavated in the 19th Century and found to extend over ninety feet beyond the chapel's original west door, under the existing baptistery and churchyard. Clearly the main area for public worship was not as important to Sir William as his Chapel. Although Altars were installed the Chapel had no formal status as a place of worship and in 1592 instructions were issued to remove and destroy the Altars. The dedication of the Chapel to the historical and Biblical St Matthew is interesting in that tradition has it that he met a martyr's death whilst praying. According to legend his severed head was taken to a monastery in France.

During the early construction period for Rosslyn Chapel the masons extensively used the Sacristy as a workman's hut and as a place of worship. The building work remained unfinished beyond the time of Sir William's death. He died in 1484 at the good old age of ninety years and was buried in the unfinished chapel. Sir William's son later completed the roof in accordance with his father's wishes. It was probably the intention that the Sacristy would be refurbished when the Chapel was nearing completion.

The Chapel was constructed in some urgency. 'Prince William, his age creeping on him first built the Sacristy as a cover for his below ground excavations for the vaults, whilst the rest of the Church was in the planning and preliminary stages.

Many would applaud such a noble ideal that the Prince should build a House for his God; few would suspect his real reason for doing so. Solomon had also built a House for the Lord; it was to hold the Ark of the Covenant ... the Treasure of Israel. All the signs are that Rosslyn also holds the secret to a treasure that was once part of the Jerusalem Temple. It will be shown that Sir William and successive Grand Masters were familiar with the location of Dagobert's gold and there is no doubt that some of the carvings at Rosslyn once understood will reveal other secrets. The arches in the Lady Chapel are festooned with small stone cubes each bearing strange symbols. Recent attempts have been made to compare them with musical notes, without real success. In the Knight Templar Temple Church in London, in that part of the church called the Round, there is an arcade of arches. These are set around the wall and between them are heads. Each head faces a differing direction and each face has a different expression. Another old Templar church is known where there are similar heads. There appears to be no comparison at Rosslyn unless it is the numerous Green Man heads. Whether it is the cubes of Rosslyn or the heads in Temple Church London there is a message to be read. Perhaps a thespian trained in the art of human expression should visit Temple Church.

In their book, 'The Hiram Key', Christopher Knight and Robert Lomas discuss finding something called the Triple Tau within the geometry of Rosslyn Chapel. The Triple Tau is used in Freemasonry and associated with the Seal of Solomon. Therein is also found the previously mentioned inscription, the translation of which reads, "Nothing is wanting but the Key", and, "If thou canst comprehend these things thou knowest enough". Within the book the authors also show a Floor Plan of the Chapel with the drawing of Solomon's Seal superimposed upon it. Immediately above the centre of the imagined seal, suspended from a ribbed arch in the Choir ceiling or roof is a Key Stone.

The authors note that the Keystone or pendant boss is in the form of an arrowhead and has the Sinclair engrailed cross upon it. Knight and Lomas think that under the flagstone directly beneath the suspended pendant is where one might find the access point to the vaults below the Chapel and that the pendant could be the 'Key that is wanting' and the treasure that is thought to be there.

Sir William St. Clair's plans were ambitious with a real sense of purpose; he was around fifty years old when the building work commenced. As well as features at Rosslyn that may be identified with Solomon's Temple the building is also modelled on the Templar Cathedral of Chartres in France; notable in the design and placing of the sacristy.

Much of the carving at Rosslyn although beautifully ornate, is just decorative stonework. There are Angels with musical instruments, others holding books and scrolls and of course green men; superb arches in the Lady Chapel and the Apprentice's Pillar is so eye-catching, so mesmerising that few have stopped to look beneath its beauty to fathom its true meaning. To unravel the mystery Sir William has bequeathed us, or rather the instructions he has left successive Knights Templar requires a knowledge that at the time was known to only a few and nowadays is lost altogether. Discovering the secret that is revealed within these pages came about not as a result of understanding of Templar or Freemasonry ceremony or ritual, but from simple observation after discovering the location of Dagobert's gold … the Treasure of Rennes-le-Chateau. Rosslyn will still have its secrets, but it is now becoming an open book and as the pages are gradually turned more secrets will come to light.

The sketch layout of the chapel (Fig 22-1) shows the five sections of the barrel-vaulted roof over the Chapel. From east to west or front to back those sections are made up of carvings of Daises, Lilies, Flowers, Roses and Stars.

The common lawn daisy (belis perennis) is a small flower with many petals, the backs of which are tipped with pink. At its centre there is a comparatively large yellow (gold) head, white surrounding gold. The Knights Templar wore a white Mantle with a large red Latin cross on the back and a comparison with the daisy is made; the daises are the gold of the Templar.

We now come to the Lilies. … In St. Matthew's gospel chapter 6, verse 28 we read ... *and why take ye thought for raiment. Consider the lilies of the field, how they grow; they toil not, neither do they spin: yet I say unto you, that even Solomon in all his glory was not arrayed like one of these.* Here Sir William St Clair uses the words of Jesus to introduce King Solomon … and Solomon built a Temple.

Next comes the Flower panel, which was mentioned earlier and which will be discussed again later. ... We now move to the Rose panel.

In the Song of Solomon chapter 2 verses 1, we read ... *I* (Solomon) *am the rose of Sharon and the lily of the valleys.* This seems to be the only mention of the rose of Sharon in scripture. It is once again Solomon and provides a link with the Lilies and a valley … the valley of the River Sals.

Turning to the last section of the Chapel roof, referred to as the 'Stars'; in fact as well as stars there are Angels, the Sun, Moon, a Dove, Jesus himself and what looks like water. We read in Luke's Gospel chapter 3, verse 21... *Now when all the people were baptised, it came to pass that Jesus also being baptised, and praying, the heavens was opened and the*

Holy Ghost descended in a bodily shape like a Dove upon Him and a voice came from Heaven.

John had been baptising people in the River Jordan when Jesus arrived and was also baptised. ... Jesus - the river and bathing. ... This reminds us of St. Nazaire by the river Sals at Rennes les Bains that is a place of bathing. The scripture references relating to the Lilies of the field and Jesus being baptised in the Jordan are familiar to most people and would not be considered unusual in Rosslyn Chapel.

A picture begins to emerge. ... The Daises say, Templar and Gold ... The Lilies and Roses point to Solomon and the Temple at Jerusalem. The Star Section tells us of Jesus and bathing. Putting the Daisy, Lilies, Roses and Star panels together the message may be read as ...

The Knight's Gold from the Temple of Solomon is in the Church of St. Nazaire Et Celse at Rennes les Bains.

That is the message Sir William has set out in his Chapel and was readily understood by successive Grand Masters. Nicolas Poussin in his paintings and Parchments says it and so does Berenger Sauniere the Priest of Rennes-le-Chateau in his Church of St Mary Magdalene.

The signs are there for all to see, the evidence is in the open and the statement is clear and unambiguous ... Dagobert's gold or the Treasure of Rennes-le-Chateau is in the Church of St. Nazaire Et Celse at Rennes les Bains.

The Flower Section in the roof of Sir William's Chapel is located between the 'Roses' and the 'Lilies' and both refer to Solomon. The arrow-headed pendant boss is suspended from the arch that separates the Roses and Flower section. Knight and Lomas have described the centre of the invisible Seal of Solomon as being on the floor of the Chapel immediately below the suspended boss. However, their configuration is only loosely supported by the Chapel layout (pillars) and although the Seal may have its place in Masonic ritual the case as set out by Knight and Lomas is not proven. The vaults probably do extend under the Chapel floor area but the pendant boss does not indicate an access at that point.

The claim is here made that the Flower section points us to the vaults beneath the Chapel. Examining this in more detail we read in Psalm 103 verse 15. ... *As for man, his days are as grass: as a flower of the field, so he flourisheth. For the wind passeth over it, and it is gone; and the place thereof shall know it no more.* ... In Matthew Chapter 6, verse 30 ... *wherefore, if God so clothe the grass (flowers) of the field, which to day is, and tomorrow is cast into the oven* ...the fireplace that is in the Sacristy.

Sir Walter Scott was born at Edinburgh in 1771 and died at Abbotsford, Roxburgh, Scotland in 1832. His epic poem, 'The Lay of the Last Minstrel'

(1805), which ran into many editions, contains details of Rosslyn Chapel that make interesting reading -

"Seemed all on fire that chapel proud,
Where Roslyn's chiefs uncoffin'd lie.
Each Baron, for a noble shroud,
Sheathed in his iron panoply.
Seemed all on fire within, around,
Deep sacristy and altars pale,
Shone every pillar foliage bound,
And glimmered all the dead men's mail.
Blazed battlement and pinnet high,
Blazed every rose-carved buttress fair -
So still they blaze when fate is nigh,
The lordly line of high St. Clair".

... And when *fate was nigh*, the fire was lit in the fireplace in the Sacristy.

Rosslyn may be a place of mystery but not of mysticism. It holds the key to immense Templar wealth, a 'key' that links ancient treasure sites. Sir Walter Scott knew that the way down into the vaults below the Chapel was via the fireplace in the Sacristy ... "Seemed all on fire that chapel proud. ... Deep sacristy. ... Pillar, foliage bound". We might wonder what else he knew. If Sir Walter Scott was not a Templar he was none the less privy to the innermost secrets of the Chapel. It is most probable the fireplace in the Sacristy was rebuilt to conceal the access to the vaults around 1736, well before Scott's time. ... Yet he knew its secrets.

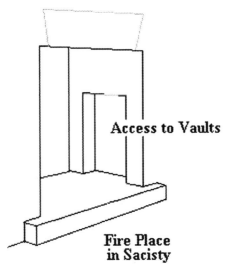

Access to Vaults

**Fire Place
in Sacisty**

Figure 22-5

There may be a traditional ecclesiastical explanation for the Daises, the Lilies, the Flowers, the Roses and the Stars that is not associated with the interpretation placed upon them by the writer of this book. It is entirely possible the reference to Flowers, the Oven and the Fireplace in the Sacristy are pure fantasy on the writer's part and that Rosslyn Chapel is no more or no less than Sir William St. Clair's dream that, ... 'It came into his mind to build a house for God's service'.

So be it.

BIBLIOGRAPHY

References made to: -

General story details relating to Berenger Sauniere from, 'The Holy Place', written by Henry Lincoln, Published by Corgi Books.

The 'Massacre at Montségur', - A History of the Albigensian Crusade. By Zoé Oldenbourg.

'Wonderful Cathar Country' by Jean-luc Aubarbier, Michel Binet and Jean-Pierre Bouchard. Published by Editions Ouest-France.

Brochure on Arques. - Courtesy Syndicate D'Initiative De Rennes les Bains.

'Rennes-le-Chateau – its Mysteries and Secrets', by Lionel and Patricia Fanthorpe, Published by Bellevue Books.

'The Treasure Maps of Rennes-le-Chateau', by Stanley James, Published by Seven Lights (Publishing).

Other Information on Rennes-le-Chateau comes from on-site material.

Scriptural references from the Holy Bible – King James Version.

The Ark of the Covenant and Manna from Heaven', an unpublished work by Geoffrey Morgan.

'The Hiram Key' by Christopher Knight and Robert Lomas, Published by Arrow Books Ltd.

Reference is made to the Encyclopaedia Britannica.

Graham Hancock's book 'The Sign and the Seal', Published by William Heinemann Ltd.

Quotation from 'Rennes-le-Chateau - All my Church' by Berenger Sauniere and Alain Feral - This is an English/French Guide brochure purchased at Rennes-le-Chateau.

Reference made to 'Nicolas Poussin – Masterclass 1594 to 1665', by Pierre Rosenberg and Veronique Damian; Published by Cassel.

Reference made to BBC *Timewatch* Programme, 'The History of a Mystery' that featured a book by Andrews and Schellenberger, entitled, 'The Tomb of God'.

Reference is made to the Rosslyn Chapel Guidebook – by the Earl of Rosslyn 1997; published by Rosslyn Chapel Trust. - Together with personal observations.

'Children's Encyclopaedia' circa 1935 Edition – edited by Arthur Mee.

Quotations from the *Authoritative Notes* and 'The Mythology of the Treasure of Rennes' by Rene Descadeillas are referred to in a letter from the Bishop of Carcassonne, translated from the French.

All drawings throughout this work are computer sketches based on photographs.

Reference is made to Map - Quillan, Alet-les-Bains, ref. 2347OT together with personal observation.

Sketches made from 'Nicolas Poussin – Masterclass 1594 to 1665', by Pierre Rosenberg and Veronique Damian. – Including, the *Guercino*, the *Louvre*, the *Chatsworth* and the *Landscape*.

The Guercino, 'The Arcadian Shepherds' is in the Galleria, Corsini, Rome.

The *Louvre* painting refers to Nicolas Poussin's 'Les Berger's d'Arcadie' currently in the Louvre, Paris, France.

The *Chatsworth* refers to Nicolas Poussin's 'Arcadian Shepherds' currently in the Duke of Devonshire's private collection at Chatsworth House, England.

The 'Landscape with three men', by Nicolas Poussin – the painting is in the Museo del Prado, Madrid.

Reproductions of the above mentioned pictures are found in 'Nicolas Poussin – Masterclass 1594 to 1665', by Pierre Rosenberg and Veronique Damian.

The sketch of the picture, 'Midas washing himself in the Pactolus', by Nicolas Poussin is found in the work, 'Poussin's Paintings a Catalogue Raisonne', by Christopher Wright.

The Brochure on Arques comes Courtesy Syndicate D'Initiative De Rennes les Bains.

The sketch of the 'Knights Tombstone' is based on an, 'Association Terre de Rhedae Tourist Information pamphlet and personal observation of the Stone in the presbytery Museum at Rennes-le-Chateau.

Rennes-le-Chateau L'Eglise, Tu le vaincras. Published by Belisane - It includes 'Plan Schematique de L'Eglise', (Plan of Church). - As well as personal observations. (English translation).

Nicolas Poussin's 'Les Bergers d'Arcadie' is reproduced by kind permission of Musée du Louvre (Service de la Communication), Paris, France.

Photographs by kind permission of –
David and Peter Morgan and Robert (Bob) Folley.
Other photographs are by the author, Geoffrey Morgan.

Geoffrey Morgan